QUEEN LESSONS

What Stand-Up Comedy Taught Me
About Dealing with Life's Hecklers and
Finding Courage in Your Queen Years

HOLLY SHAW

Queen Lessons
Copyright © 2025 by Holly Shaw

All rights reserved. Without limiting the rights under the copyright reserved above, no part of this publication may be reproduced, stored in, or introduced into a retrieval system, or transmitted in any form or by any means (electronic, mechanical, photocopying, recording, or otherwise) without prior written permission.

For permission requests, please contact: holly@performersandcreatorslab.com

ISBN: 978-1-7362024-2-5 paperback
ISBN: 978-1-7362024-3-2 e-book
ISBN: 978-1-7362024-4-9 hardcopy

Written by Holly Shaw
Content editing by Stephanie Edd
Developmental editing by Abigail Keyes
Original front cover photo by Aaron Fagerstrom
Original back cover photo by Nick Larson
Cover Art and Interior Book Design by Heidi Sutherlin

Published in the United States by:
Performers & Creators Lab
Oakland, California

www.performersandcreatorslab.com

Printed in the United States of America

Dedication

This book is dedicated to my inner Nice Girl.

May she rest in peace.

Table of Contents

The Premise: Your Soul is Secretly Evolving 1

The Setup: A Comedian, a Wise Woman,
and Earthquake Woman Walk into a Bar 15

CHAPTER I - The Queen Years 21

CHAPTER II: Attention: Playing the Fool 43

CHAPTER III - Desire: From Blind Ambition
to Finding Your Point of View 65

CHAPTER IV - Boldness: Asking for the Gig 87

CHAPTER V - Persistence: Popping the Room or Eating It 109

CHAPTER VI - Attention: Waging a War 127

CHAPTER VII - Shamelessness: Working the Crowd 143

CHAPTER VIII - Honesty: Killing It 163

CHAPTER IX - Loyalty: Staying True to Yourself 181

CHAPTER X - All Your Courage: Dealing with Hecklers 199

CHAPTER XI - That's My Time: Shining a Light on Others 225

CHAPTER XII - Attention: Wearing the Crown 241

The Punchline 253

Murmuring at You from Inside My Sleeping Bag 257

Acknowledgements 261

Biography 263

Women Comedians to the World

Stand up and speak truth to strangers

Practice this

The boldness

The asking of your presence

*Tell the stories that bubble up in the
company of your closest friends*

*The ones that make you laugh so hard
until no sound comes out*

Tell those stories and let them gawk

At the audacity of you

If it gets awkward, just let it be awkward

You are not responsible for anyone's comfort

You are only responsible for the unflinching narrative

Of your fabulous, wicked, fruitful life…

The Premise
Your Soul is Secretly Evolving

It's a balmy night in late August, and I'm standing on a small stage facing a sea of about four hundred people or so… we lost count after the show started and people started creeping over the ropes and sliding silently into any space available, too excited not to be a part of this grand finale. This night is an epic ending to an event that was bestowed as a crown of hope during a worldwide pandemic. I am beyond thrilled, but a part of me can't help but marvel at how I got here. It was never in my plans.

We're a crowd of people perched on a waterfront patio set up like an outdoor comedy club. The dynamic swells of the water glisten behind me, on stage like a backdrop of dark jewels. *The Comedy Edge*. This is set at Brooklyn Basin, one of Oakland's newest parks, designed to inspire awe: a sprawling oval the size of a football field thrust out over the water of the Bay between Oakland and Alameda. Visitors roller-skate, walk, and picnic with their friends on the swaths of grass or oversized wooden chaise lounge chairs. At night, sometimes renegade DJs set up their equipment to inspire spontaneous dance parties. The architects were wise to keep it simple, leaving only enough of the old buildings—a slice of a wall here with a striking window, a steel archway framing the center. These minimalistic touches give hints at the structures that once existed without dominating the space—the sunsets in crimson and burnt sienna meeting the crisp blue of the water are the main attraction.

Over the last three years, The Comedy Edge has grown a huge following with many regulars coming for the exciting and diverse lineups and the beautiful outdoor setting. There's Trish and Ash, the adventurous couple who flood their Instagram feed with images of their latest restaurant excursion or comedy show. They have been to at least 10 shows here and have gradually become my real friends. Sher and her boyfriend also come a lot, because of health concerns they only do outdoor activities. Then there's Sami and his wife who drive all the way up from Santa Cruz for these shows… and of course my sister and her friend Liza are regulars; although tonight my sister has also brought along my fourteen-year-old nephew, River. Normally, minors under 18 can't attend these shows, but tonight we've made an exception. Tonight, we are all here to celebrate the end.

On this particular night I can feel a bit of moisture on my fingers as I gently grip the microphone. I can no longer tell what is moisture from the air and what is sweat. It all blends into one lubricant for the evening's comedic revelry. I have just finished my regular set, the laughter of my closing joke lingering like a kiss. Now because it's the last night, because everyone expects it about as much as you expect a toast from the best man at a wedding, I go nostalgic and launch into a story. I feel like I'm giving a tribute, or rather a eulogy:

"Many years ago, I was on a plane going from Reno to San Francisco and we hit some turbulence. The plane began to shake side to side violently… I start to feel anxious so I looked to the windows. I figured if I can see something—a mountain, some bit of sky, a cloud in the distance—

then I'll know where I am in space. I'll feel better. But there's nothing to see except for clouds pressed right up next to the glass. I can't see two feet out the window. And then all of the sudden the plane drops about a hundred feet."

I hit the top of the microphone and drop into a crouch. Some people in the audience jump at the drop like they feel it in their bodies, too. Everyone goes still, wondering what happens next.

When the global pandemic hit, this waterfront patio became one of the premiere venues for shows. Not only was it ideal because it was outdoors with ample airflow, covered by a two-story high ceiling, and plenty of space to social distance, but it was also just sublimely beautiful. The views and the architecture were magnificent. Producing this comedy show here Saturday after Saturday for three years, gathering people to laugh together and to listen together felt somehow... hopeful.

I slowly rise from my crouched position and continue the story, "My heart was beating so fast and everyone on the plane just started going nuts, people crying out like, 'Gladys, are you okay?!'" the audience chuckles.

"And I'm thinking to myself that I really hope that everyone can... shut the fuck up right now because they're stressing me out!" People giggle at my unexpected turn from concern to annoyance, grateful for the break in tension.

"Then I notice that the man next to me is crying. Like really ugly crying." I act out a man ugly crying. "And I feel bad for him so I tell him, 'Listen, we're gonna be okay. This is uncomfortable, but planes are built for this. We are going to be just fine.'" My tone was comforting.

"Then all of a sudden, the plane drops again!" I hit the microphone and drop a few inches. The audience hangs in silence, the water behind me laps suddenly, making a hungry slurping sound as if trying to add levity.

"But this time when the plane drops," I continue, "I put my hands in the air… and I put my feet in the air and I go, 'Wheeeee!'" The audience erupts into delighted laughter.

"The man next to me kind of cry-chuckles." I act out a grown man laughing and crying at the same time. "And I say, 'You should try it!' so the man puts his hands and feet in the air and tries it: 'Wheee!' And then it starts to catch on. The people behind us start doing it, the people in front of us catch on, too, and eventually half the plane is riding a roller coaster during the worst night of their lives."

I pause here and look over to DJ Styles. He has been with the show for two of the three seasons, adding such a wonderful element of playfulness through the lively walk-up music hand-picked for each comic. Sometimes as he listens to a comedian's jokes, he'll get an idea for a song that would make a hilarious walk-off song for them. If someone references some wild night they had, they might have to walk-off stage to Rick James's *Super Freak*. A comedian has jokes about discovering their bisexuality: Katy Perry's *I Kissed a Girl*.

An exceptionally tall Black man Oakland native, and a high school teacher, Styles is like a gentle giant with the heart of a puppy and the musical intuition of a rave wizard. Styles has become a fixture at the Comedy Edge, sitting just off to the side of the stage with his laptop and sound board, laughing and fist pumping enthusiastically for the comics and often getting the last laugh with a song.

In order to manage such a large show, I've hired a rotating crew of comedians to help me set up and take tickets at the door. Styles is the only person who is with me at every show, so we've developed a rating system to describe how shows are going. We've rarely had what you could consider a truly bad show at this venue, so most shows fall into one of two categories: *Sparkly* is when a show is so good it feels sparkly. There's a lightness in the air. A sparkly night is a good time, satisfying, a job well done.

But then there are the *shimmer nights*. These are rare. A shimmer night is when it's so good that when you look out across the audience the air shimmers with harmony all night long. It's a vibe that feels like, well, *love*. When I'm on stage performing during a shimmer night, it feels like my words are impactful, like I can feel them leaving me and slicing through the air. Maybe it's some ghost of inspiration that blows through on the Bay breeze, or maybe it's just the particular chemistry of those comics and that particular audience but whatever it is, it's magical.

I look at Styles knowingly. Tonight is a shimmery night. The most shimmery of shimmery. I can feel us both savoring it. Wanting to lock it away for a day in the near future when this show no longer exists. I am relishing this final performance on this particular stage and taking my sweet time to land this plane. I finally continue:

"Eventually the plane lands and we all get home safe." I pause. "So, I'm telling you this story because I know that right now, the world and everything going on in it—the pandemic, the violence, the politics, the confusion—feels like a bumpy airplane ride. It's terrifying and we can't see two feet out the window and we don't know when it's going to end. We don't know who is going to land this plane. But we need the artists, we need comedians to make us laugh, to lighten the mood, change our perspectives, and help us get through it."

The audience rewards me with applause. I'm relieved. Sometimes this "moral of the story" moment is too saccharine for a comedy audience. But tonight, it's clearly what's called for. "We need the comedians to save us!"

I wait for the swell of cheering to crest and fall before I continue, "And I think of all the comedians and artists that I know—" I look to the back of the room where the comics on the show that night are all standing and watching—"I just think…" I pause for effect. "Oh, we're fucked!" The surprise hits the crowd and their mouths open to let out a shimmer of delight that rushes up my body and makes my head buzz with gratification.

I feel love, nothing but love. I grab the tail end of their merriment and push the energy higher while they're still with me: "That's why we need everybody! We are like the plane. We are built for this and we will get through it together, but we need all of us. We need all of you! We need the bus drivers, the bartenders, the teachers, the scientists, the dominatrix, the underwater basket weavers, and the weed delivery person. We need everyone to be creative. We need everyone to land this plane! So, thank you for coming out for three years and supporting live comedy. Thank you for sharing in this lighter, more hopeful space with us. Thank you!"

The audience rises in ovation. Trish's lip is quivering and her eyes are misty as she pounds her hands together. My nephew is pumping his fist in the air and yelling, "Go aunty!" And as all the noise washes over me, it dawns on me: This show was my airplane through this storm that was the pandemic. This show has carried me.

Over the last three years, I've worked so hard to produce this show. I tackled it like it was my full-time job, doing non-stop marketing, booking, preparation to make every week special. I came every Saturday *four hours early* to rearrange the tables and chairs, haul and set up the lighting and speakers, and then I would run around all throughout the show making sure every guest had what they needed, that every comedian was supported and ready to go. I'd look at my pedometer at the end of the night and would discover I had walked twenty thousand steps! Every Sunday after a show I would go fully horizontal, exhausted and just trying to recover. I had worked myself so hard that I had it in my head that *I* was carrying this show; but as the sound of the audience travelled out across Brooklyn Basin, carried over the Bay waters by the wind, I realized

I was just a steward to something magical. The whole time I thought I was carrying it, but really the magic of comedy was carrying *me*.

That night after that grand finale of The Comedy Edge, I marveled at how I got there. I didn't plan for that. Producing a major comedy show wasn't on my vision board. Heck, even stand-up comedy had only recently made it onto my vision board...

Vision Boards Make Fools of Us All

Vision boards. What do you think of 'em? I've always had mixed feelings myself. I like the idea: *Let's really focus and envision what we want in life. Let's be deliberate creators!* But then I feel somewhat silly with the scissors in my hands and my fingertips sticky with Elmer's Glue. I think to myself, *Yeah, but is this really going to work?*

My son's paternal grandfather, Phil, or *Gpa Phil*, as we call him, has often been a spiritual advisor to my son and me. Quirky, loving, and a total goofball, he never seems to lose his sense of adventure. But he can also be candid and straight to the point when you need him to be.

I remember years ago, right after the new year began, proudly showing Gpa Phil my vision board: An image of some comedian facing a huge crowd in a fancy theatre, a fairy tale cottage in the woods, names of comedy clubs I wanted to perform at carefully cobbled together from magazine words. I'm not particularly skilled at arts and crafts, but I was proud of the aesthetically pleasing combination of aspirational cut-out pictures I had arranged on a poster board. Gpa Phil wasn't particularly impressed. "You know your spirit doesn't really care anything about that?"

"Huh?" I said, confused.

"In some ways it really doesn't matter what you do with yourself in this lifetime," he said. "Your soul is learning lessons, whatever you end up achieving or not achieving. Your soul couldn't give two shits about your 'goals.'" And with that, he sniffed, hiked up his pants, and started searching up places for us to go to dinner.

I have returned to this idea from Gpa Phil regularly ever since and I find that I am comforted by it. Have you ever considered that while you are painstakingly planning your goals, cutting out little pieces of magazine and pasting it onto your vision board, that your soul is secretly evolving in ways that have nothing to do with it? No matter what your intellect or your ego is steering you towards—the whole time your soul is just hanging out, watching, and taking notes (not studiously; more like doodling hearts on a scratch pad). Your soul is having its own journey.

When I randomly decided to pop into an open mic, it was nudging me towards an art form that would challenge and fulfill me. When I randomly agreed to take a meeting with a friend of a friend who owned a cool venue, my soul was giving me the space to produce *The Comedy Edge*. Maybe you've seen it too: you randomly decide to take up dancing lessons, and your soul nudges you towards the style that's going to challenge you the most. You randomly decide to go to a new place for a walk on a bright sunny day, perhaps your soul is planning an adorable meet-cute for you.

I love this idea of my soul secretly evolving, nudging me around and doing its own sacred, important things. It makes me feel better when my vision board doesn't put out or when I don't end the year with all my goals tied up with a neat pretty bow. When I start to compare myself to someone else and feel inferior, I think, *Yeah, but my soul's got other plans*. If things aren't going the way I think they should, then it's a lovely idea to imagine that some other part of me has got this, or at the very least is growing and learning lessons along the way.

We don't always see or feel our soul's movement. In the busyness of our lives, our to-do lists, our caretaking of friends and families, we can lose touch with our soul. Sometimes it can feel as if I'm standing in one place. But the soul's movement is as deceptive as a smooth airplane ride.

THE PREMISE

I feel like I'm going nowhere but 12 hours later I arrive in a whole other part of the world. My soul doesn't always let me in on their plan or what things mean. For example, what does the disastrous lunch or the mind-numbing job I feel stuck in have to do with my self-growth? But that's the thing: You don't have to know what it's for; sometimes you just have to trust you're on the airplane ride.

Sometimes I try to peek behind the curtain to see what gifts they've amassed back there. I like to understand what I'm learning so that when it feels like I'm standing still, I know that I'm not. Even as I'm telling the same jokes this month that I did last month, trying to punch up my set, doing the same shows with the same people, I'd like to think there is movement happening in my soul.

This book is based on the premise that your soul and my soul are secretly evolving. And if my glimpses tell me anything, it's that mine has changed a lot through the practice of performing stand-up comedy. What jewels have I amassed from hours of open mics, showcases, waiting in the wings, and learning to make large audiences laugh at my whim like I'm a conductor of a raucous laugh orchestra? What have I accomplished by the dozens of small deaths I have died in the awkward silences? How has it shaped me? The persistent hecklers, the shady bookers, the dirty underbelly of show business—What could my soul possibly want to do with all of that shite?

My soul is secretly evolving all the time no matter what is going on and the queen years are for many a time of taking stock of what's changed in our lives. This book is an attempt to track down the changes and flesh them out into something resembling wisdom. Let's get into it.

Story and Poetry: Speaking in the Soul's Language

Throughout this book, I sometimes track my soul's movements through stories and poetry because these are the soul's languages. Also, sometimes, I reach all the way back to my childhood stories. Stories are how we find meaning in the world. Our life and the lessons in it are made of stories. So I reflect on the stories of my time in comedy as well as in life. Sometimes, to track the soul's slow progression we need a bigger sample size. Every queen knows that she didn't become the woman she is today fully formed with no backstory. It is our past that shapes us, angers us, infuses us with our own desires, needs, and methods for getting those needs met. Childhood memories are a must. The lessons I'm sharing with you are a harvest of the entire soul's journey from the maiden to the mother to the *queen*.

Sometimes, to get to the things that are hard to put into words, poetry appears—or when things just get way too tense and way too dark… a joke. The laughter cracks us wide open and lets the medicine in. The medicine that frees us from shame, fear, or simply lifts us out of our own self-centered misery. Laughter makes us present in the moment and softens the blow of truth. So I'll try to make this medicine as buoyant and enjoyable as possible, no painful shots to the arm—I promise. Only tinctures and potions for you to sip at your free will.

Stories, poetry, jokes… I know this all sounds like *a lot*. And let me tell you, this book didn't come together easily! As unwieldy as a basket of puppies, these stories scrambled over each other, fell asleep on me in odd positions, and at times escaped and hid under the couch, whimpering. But that is what happens when you give birth to a litter. You either get a super-power vacuum cleaner or you get used to the mess. Regardless of the mess, fostering your stories and unearthing your soul's journey is immensely satisfying.

Maybe you aren't a stand-up comedian, but regardless of what you've chosen to do with yourself, you, too, have a soul that is secretly evolving. It is my hope that by listening to mine, you might begin to hear yours.

THE PREMISE

What have they been secretly doing? What impulses have borne you the fruit of wisdom? And which ones have you ignored?

We can only ignore our soul's needs, desires, impulses, and cravings until they begin to bubble and burn inside of us. When we find ourselves creeping into mid-life anything we've ignored is coming for us.

We must listen or risk burning up inside.

And it's going to take all parts of us to do it.

Dance Challenge! at the Comedy Edge we'd do intermission giveaways which would often result in a dance-off as audience members were inspired to shake a move for a free gift, often just a bottle of wine or some chocolate.

Performing on stage at the Comedy Edge (photo Jim McCambridge)

Early days social distanced tables at the Comedy Edge
(photo Jim McCambridge)

THE PREMISE

Wheeee!" telling the airplane story on stage at the Comedy Edge (photo Aaron Fagerstrom).

An audience member jumps on stage to dance with me and comedian, Wonder Dave, during a dance challenge.

QUEEN LESSONS

At the Comedy Edge with comedians Steven Asifo,
Jaren George, Ryan Goodcase, Aivy Cordova

Night falls at Brooklyn Basin and I am
illuminated by artfully hung spotlights.

The Setup
A Comedian, a Wise Woman, and Earthquake Woman Walk into a Bar

There are three different women inside of me... at least.

I don't know how you run your mind, but mine is like an intergenerational improv troupe with different parts of me chiming in and no one in particular running the show. You wouldn't necessarily know it to talk to me, but I am spilling over with personalities all wanting their time in the spotlight. Writing this book, three of them began to emerge as champions for the queen lessons.

If being a semi-regular participant in psychotherapy and working with people as a hypnotherapist has taught me anything, it's that each of us has archetypes within. Defining these archetypes can help us hear their guidance more clearly. I've definitely made allies with mine. So let me introduce you to these ladies, who will reappear throughout this book.

Earthquake Woman

All of us queens have to develop some kind of protection. Some fierce part of ourselves that rises to the occasion to save us when we need it. For many of us, we've realized the knight on a white horse isn't coming to save us, so we create our own. For me, her name is Earthquake Woman.

Earthquake Woman is righteous anger. Women don't feel like they're allowed to get angry—we might be accused of hysteria. So what do we do? We suppress it. We push it down, push it down, until there's no room left for anything else and it erupts when we lose control. This is Earthquake Woman. She's filled to the brim with rage like hot lava. It's the kind of anger only a woman can know, forged by a lifetime of injustices, but it can also be a great fuel for desire. The anger bubbles and spits sometimes, warning those around me to watch out. You never know when Earthquake Woman is going to blow.

But Earthquake Woman is a powerful force, misunderstood, and ready for a promotion. Her anger may be destructive, but it all depends on where you end her story. In reality she's just an underpaid employee clearing the emotional brush of your stunted, nutrient-deficient relationships.

The Comedian

Being a comedian is really fun because I get to say things onstage that I would likely never say in the company of most people. For instance,

> *My pussy has become a halfway house for emotionally unavailable men. Many have been through this program.*

The Comedian doesn't just give me a license to say what I want. She provides relief from tension, relief from pain, relief from the heaviness and precocity of religion, reverence, and taking myself too seriously. The Comedian helps Earthquake Woman let out some of the anger and turn it into laughter. Every woman I know cultivates a cackle as she enters her queen years, a real throaty, loud, gleeful, witchy laugh best served with her head thrown back in abandon—It makes the sound travel farther and scares off the patriarchy.

The Wise Woman

The Wise Woman gets out of the shower arms dripping with proverbs. She speaks in poetry and riddles and asks a lot of questions. She wears her subconscious on her sleeve. She is kind but not always nice. She's a connection to what's waiting for us in the great beyond. She can channel your dead father or the divine creative spirit. She could channel the squirrel outside your window if you really wanted her to. Just don't get her drunk or she'll channel people you don't want to hear from. She's exceptionally horny because she's in tune with desire and creativity and can intuitively sense where energy is flowing. She can tell when your lover is in love with someone else. She can also save you from staying with the wrong partner.

Every woman I know has a Wise Woman within her, whether she's accustomed to listening to her or not. When a child gets lost, they look for a woman in the crowd to help them; they feel instinctively that she'll know what to do. The Wise Woman—the one who knows what to do—exists in all of us.

Just as a queen's court might have knights to fight off the dragons, a court jester to entertain, and a high priestess to advise, I have Earthquake Woman, the Comedian, and the Wise Woman. All of these characters play a part in the makings of a queen.

A woman isn't initiated into womanhood without recognizing that she has to suppress parts of herself in different settings. Sometimes her inner Comedian is just what she needs to break the tension in awkward moments but also cracks inappropriate jokes at work, or the Wise Woman is needed to talk a friend down from a ledge but isn't as welcomed at family gatherings. And Earthquake Woman? Well, she's hardly accepted anywhere. That's why she rumbles and spits. They say little eruptions help keep the temperature down inside... Well... We'll see.

A Comedian, a Wise Woman, and an Earthquake Woman walk into a bar. The Comedian cracks jokes for anyone who will listen. The Wise woman reads everyone's relationship auras without asking. Earthquake Woman gets thrown out for starting a fight.

As I was groping for a way to tackle this very tenuous topic of women who are stepping into their queen years (i.e. those years starting for most in their forties, but for some as young as their thirties, marking the beginning of a woman's transformation into her true prime of power and creativity), it was clear to me this book would need to look at this topic through multiple lenses. At the time I began, I was desperately seeking the words and the inspiration to feel purposeful and good about getting older as a woman in this world. It wasn't my intellect that needed saving. It was my soul. So, this book is meant to simmer and soar, dip, spit, and splash across mind *and* spirit.

As we get older as women, we are naturally angrier and all of the injustices we've endured start bubbling up to the surface. We become more intuitive and have gathered wisdom. And we can't talk about the horrors, the trials, the gifts, and the honest-to-goddess blessings of this period in our lives without a damn good sense of humor. We finally know who we are and have carved out some sense of self-confidence. And yet this is also when the world starts to ignore us?

We can either laugh or cry at this injustice. I prefer to cackle.

All three of the women inside of me joined me as I sat down to write this book: Earthquake Woman straddles a chair and breathes hot breath on the back of my neck, the Wise Woman hovers over my shoulder and finds a sensitive pressure point in which to massage me with her thumb, and the Comedian bounces wildly on an exercise ball, eager to get started. All three of them start bossing me around.

Pardon me—all three just leaned forward to remind me that they are being assertive, not bossy, and would I please set aside the patriarchal messaging so we can write this book together?

It's tough. There's a lot of conditioning. But I'll do my best.

CHAPTER I

The Queen Years

People call me a cougar. Roar! I guess I'm of cougar age.
But I don't feel the roar! I don't feel like a cougar.
I feel more like a big mama cat with distended nipples.

It was New Year's Eve in Ukiah, an adorable small town in Northern California. The night was cool enough for a coat but not punishing. I was flying high from a performance and was just going to drop my stuff off so I could skip across the street to dance with some other comics at a local bar. I was loading up my car when a woman ran up to me, a bit breathless, and asked, "Is it too late to get a scarf?"

I had a really great performance that night. The whole thing was in the pocket and the audience laughed exactly when I wanted them to. I can still remember some of the faces of the women in the audience throwing their heads back in laughter, and the men pounding their hands on the table with mirth. It was an uproarious night, ridiculously fun and connected.

I had brought some new merchandise to this gig to sell after the show, including these pretty cashmere scarves, one of my mantras from my show printed on them in soft gray lettering:

Ask for what you want.

I told audiences that it was a reminder for them that they could return throughout the new year, a reminder to speak up and ask for what they wanted more often. The scarves themselves came in pink and red—my signature colors. After the show I had the chance to sell some at a back table and for the first time I really understood what that exchange was about. It was less about the money and more about just giving people an opportunity to connect with me. I welcomed that connection and cherished it, even now after I had already packed up and this pretty, dark-haired woman approached me.

"Is it too late to buy one?" she asked. I could see her clutching a handful of bills and shifting her weight nervously like she was anxious to get back to wherever she had just come from. She had dark brown hair—a knowing eye told me she had just had her roots done—chunky glasses in the vein of Mel Robbins, and was wearing black from head to toe except for a tiny shimmer of sequins peeking out from under her jacket at the collar. True to the New Year's Eve trend, I noticed that a lot of ladies had rocked the sequin outfits tonight. She looked to be in her late forties or early fifties.

"No problem, I can still grab you one!" I said as I threw my suitcase into the trunk and unzipped it to show her the options.

"I really wanted to stop at your table earlier and buy one but my husband wouldn't let me," she admitted.

"Okay well..." I paused, taking in her words.

Her husband wouldn't let her?!" Earthquake Woman grumbled.

There was so much I wanted to say and I felt my mind speeding through a rush of scenarios. I had to remember though that this woman knew me as the Comedian. It might not go over well to give in to my curiosity by letting Wise Woman ask questions or let Earthquake Woman have her say.

Instead, I kept it light. "I'm just so glad you spotted me out here and came over! Would you like one in pink or red?"

CHAPTER I - THE QUEEN YEARS

The woman chose a red scarf and I asked her if she would like to share a hug and we embraced briefly. As she rushed back to the car that was waiting for her, I called out to her, "Hey! Good for you! You asked for what you wanted!" I don't know if she heard me say it, but it felt right. She jumped into a waiting car and it zoomed off.

My husband wouldn't let me.

Those words rang in my ears the rest of that night, the next day, and for weeks afterward. It cemented what I was already coming to understand. Maybe sometimes I didn't feel like I belonged in the world of stand-up comedy. Even though I was doing well and getting booked, it definitely seemed like some of the younger comics or the blatantly sexist and ageist bookers didn't want me in their world. But this woman had reminded me that there was an entire planet of women out there, especially those in their queen years, that not only wanted to hear me do stand-up, but actually needed it.

What Do I Mean by Queen Years?

Your queen years begin right in that transition when your fertility[1] is waning but your senior years still feel ahead of you, when you wonder what comes next in life.[1] You're not exactly young, but you're not old, either. Maybe you're done having children, or you never had kids and are

---

[1] I speak from the viewpoint of a cisgender woman, so you'll see me sometimes mention hormonal fluctuations that come from menopause. I'm no expert but I hear from transgender women that although they don't exactly experience menopause, they too can experience menopause-like symptoms caused by fluctuating levels of estrogen from their HRT. While some of this book talks about the physical challenges of these queen years, many other things I talk about include the social challenges of being a woman, with which trans women can commiserate. They endure these same challenges as well as new and ever more difficult ones.

wondering if it's finally too late. Perhaps you can't get pregnant anymore and you're thrilled. The queen years often start after a woman's kids are out of the house, but not necessarily. Some of us queens never had kids or waited and had them later.

As a queen, you get pissed when AARP starts sending you stuff in the mail, but you also have no patience for uncomfortable shoes. Your hormones begin to drop. If you color your hair, you start checking the boxes for phrases like, "extra strong gray coverage." Your body is changing (to put it politely) and your skin suddenly looks... *different*. Any injuries or small problems in your health tend to bark really loudly and you start researching things like collagen and anti-inflammatories and asking the internet, "Does fasting really work for menopause?"

You see pictures of yourself and you still look like you but just kind of...tired. And inside you might feel some combination of grief for what's no longer available for you (babies, partnership fantasies, aspirational careers, feats of your youth) and relief that those years are over. You feel a mixture of many emotions: sadness, regret, freedom, and anger—wow a lot of anger... leaving you wondering, *Why am I suddenly so pissed off?!* (Cue Earthquake Woman.)

Regardless of how you feel about it, the foreboding call of perimenopause comes for many of our bodies either way: Hormones change and we begin to cut free from the societal ties that want to hold us to what we *should* do and begin living life exactly how we want. I think of it as a time when a woman just says "fuck a bunch of all this" and starts living more truthfully.

How often do you hear a woman say the menopausal journey is inspiring? Perhaps not as much as you should, but beneath the body changes, the dramatic relationship shifts, the emotional upheaval that can at times make you feel like a naughty adolescent, is a fantastic metamorphosis of body and soul. A beautiful change! Oh dang, did I just

CHAPTER I - THE QUEEN YEARS

invoke Nurse DeeDee from fifth grade sex-ed class? The problem is, it doesn't always feel so charming when you're going through it.

People love to compare it to a butterfly in a cocoon, but what no one tells you is that it's more like getting your hands on one of those sea monkey kits. Remember those novelty aquarium pets? Supposedly you just add water and nutrients and, voila, you are the caretaker of fascinating creatures! But just like perimenopause, the transformation isn't always as cute or simple as that. All too often it's more likely the things squirm around for a few minutes while you step away from the glass, so you miss the whole show, only to find them all floating to the top like a funky shrimp soup. I sometimes also feel like a funky shrimp soup. And that's not a new feeling.

I remember going through puberty in middle school and often feeling miserable, so burdened by the weight of my feelings that I just wanted to roll up into a ball, disappear underneath the leaves, and break down into compost. I recognize that same impetus now, only I understand it comes from the very real sensation that changes are happening. If you can just hold on tight through the funky-shrimp-soup phase you might be able to survive long enough to turn over your outsides, and bust out something gorgeous. Perimenopause is an awkward, inconvenient, and, at times, beautiful transformation that a woman goes through on her way to becoming her most powerful and creative self.

In order to survive the big changes happening, it takes grit to stick with yourself and a willingness to transmute anger into something useful. It takes a whole lot of patience as you navigate how to speak your truth, get your needs met, and be heard in a world that has decided to stop listening to you.

So, you see, the boldness and the raw honesty that was required to become a stand-up comedian could not have come at a better time for me than my queen years. Because whether we like it or not, it's a comedian's job to say what's really happening—like the other night at the Starry Plough....

Time Makes You Bolder

It was a warm night in Berkeley, California at the Starry Plough, a venue that hosts one of my favorite weekly open mics. About a hundred performers of all kinds show up every week—musicians, comedians, poets, singer/songwriters—to put their name in a hat in order to get a chance to perform. It's a real intergenerational scene: Many young students from the nearby UC Berkeley come through, as well as middle-aged hipsters and old hippies, including the local poet, *Joan of Art*, and a little impish old man with a long white beard known as *the Professor*. I've never seen the Professor actually perform, but he enjoys heckling the comedians, dancing around to the music, and generally providing a sideshow throughout a good portion of the night until he adorably passes out in a chair in the back corner.

The Starry Plough is a real community bar. Any day of the week there's different kinds of music and sometimes social dancing. With its wooden floors, scattering of tables, and a small stage light with colorful warm lights, it creates a homey vibe for artists to come and do their thing. Beer, wine and kombucha are served. On the wall is a quote from 1907 by the Irish trade union leader, James Connolly:

> *No Revolutionary movement is complete without its poetic expression. If such a movement has caught hold of the imagination of the masses, they will seek a vent in song for the aspirations, fears, and hopes of the loves and hatreds engendered by the struggle. Until the movement is marked by the joyous, defiant singing of revolutionary songs, it lacks one of the most distinctive marks of a popular revolutionary movement; it is the dogma of the few and not the faith of the multitude.*

CHAPTER I - THE QUEEN YEARS

I was looking at this quote while the act on stage painfully made their way through their song. There were two young men up there, *probably no older than my kid*, I thought. One of them was sitting down playing a guitar while the other one sort of leaned gingerly on the mic stand and sang. Or attempted to. They were objectively bad. Not only were they both singing off key—in different keys no less!—but they also appeared to not know the words. And most interestingly, they were singing *Landslide* by Fleetwood Mac, the lyrics of which are not an obvious pick for young men just trying to grow in their moustaches:

Well, I've been 'fraid of changin'

'Cause I've built my life around you

But time makes you bolder

Even children get older

And I'm gettin' older, too

The crowd of fellow musicians at the Starry Plough at first tensed up at the blatant torture of this well-known song, but they eventually softened. Everyone has to start somewhere and this open mic is known to host talent with a wide range of experience. People began chiming in with the lyrics in the *correct* key.

"Oh no, oh no" I thought to myself, "Please don't make me go after these boys." I knew my number was coming up soon, but I couldn't remember when exactly. I just knew if I went up after these guys, I would have to roast them. It's just too easy. When the boys finally finished the applause for them was warm and genuinely supportive.

The host, Johnny, went up on stage and handled it exactly as a good host of any mixed open mic should. "Thank you, Arrow and Duck!" (Side note: I don't make these names up. Berkeley parents do.)

27

"You know," Johnny continued, "It takes a lot of courage to get up here and perform in front of a room full of people so I'm super impressed you guys! Keep coming back! Okay! So now for our next act, coming to the stage, a regular here at the Starry Plough, always hilarious, always fun, give it up for one of my favorites, Holly Shaw!"

Oh shit okay well here we go, I thought. I looked around the room for something else to get my mind off the boys and glanced at the James Connolly quote as I passed it. *Yes,* I thought. *I'll start there.*

Johnny gave me a fist bump as I climbed onstage, grabbed the mic out of the stand, and turned towards the audience, regarding the expectant faces. Arrow and Duck were still getting high fives from their college buddies, so I waited for the commotion to die down before I spoke.

"You know, it's really good to be here at the Starry Plough." I looked over at James Connoly's words. "The Starry Plough and this mic in particular is one of my favorite places to be. This is where I wanna be when fascism takes us all... because it's coming for us." I nodded somberly. "But you know what I think? Art is revolutionary and it will save us." There was a smattering of cheers at this off to the left so I leaned into the idea.

"Yes, art will save us. Music! Music will save us!" And then I paused and couldn't help myself. "Well, maybe not Arrow and Ducky, though." The shocked, open mouths nearly sucked the air out of the room. I wasn't sure which way this was going to go, but I immediately looked at Arrow and Duck's faces to get a read if I went too far. They didn't seem hurt. In fact, they were smiling delightedly. They looked thrilled at the extra attention. Then the crowd relaxed, gave in to the hooting and howling, and agreed to let me roast these guys' struggling performance.

I continued, "I'm just sayin'..." I directed the next part to Arrow and Duck, "I have to poke fun at you guys a little bit. I'm so impressed that you guys decided to practice zero times!" The laughter fluttered up at this and fell back down. I sobered up my tone. "But in truth I want you to know," I placed my hand over my heart and looked at them with a motherly gaze, "You guys made me tear up a bit."

Someone in the audience said, "Awww" and I nodded.

"That song. I was just like, 'Awww, look at these two young men who decided to sing a song from the perspective of a middle-aged woman!" This made Arrow and Duck's bodies fold over and wiggle sideways as they slapped their knees in laughter. I was filled with satisfaction. It's a devious pleasure to get away with all of this roasting. It definitely is a new edge for me: not being "nice."

But hey, James Connolly urged us to remember that any movement is "marked by the joyous, defiant singing of revolutionary songs." Though he gave no instruction to comedians who would mock those who sing off key.

If he only knew how far I've come from being a "Nice Girl" to get to this point.

The Nice Girl

When I started doing stand-up comedy many people reacted incredulously, even saying they never thought of me as the "comic type."

I get it. I'm sincere, not sharp. More earnest than sarcastic. People see me on stage telling jokes and they think I must have always been witty, but that couldn't be farther from the truth. For as long as I can remember, I was always a "Nice Girl." Growing up in Indiana, I was trained by midwestern culture to be polite. And not just polite, but obedient.

Indiana is part of the Bible belt. People in my hometown of Southport, the southside of Indianapolis, loved Jesus and basketball in equal parts. I was curious about religion and would often tag along with my friends on Sundays to taste test their religious ceremonies. Jehovah's Witnesses, Baptist, Catholic all were hugely more interesting than my own, Presbyterian, but with all of them I felt like a tourist. I'd wander through and try to live like the locals: I got baptized once just because they were doing my friend and they offered me one—guess it was buy-one-get-one-free on baptisms that day. My mom was furious when she found out she missed it—but I just shrugged and went to lay down afterwards. All that holy spirit had given me a headache.

I would also devour *The Watchtower* magazines lying around my friend's house as though they were science-fiction novels, and I marveled at their prophecies. The Catholics never did let me try the wafer and wine at communion, though I got back at them by purchasing a large bag of wafers in college from this place that sold them in bulk. Me and my friends would get high and munch on Jesus.

No matter what religion I was sampling I always felt like it didn't quite fit. It didn't quite resonate with what god felt like to me. I felt like I had a direct line to the spirit and everyone else's version was overdoing it just a little. So, I did not fall in line with the Indiana passion for Jesus, and basketball was even more boring than the long sermons.

Stamping my religion passport at different churches and congregations around town seemed to appease everyone who cared about my soul (my parents really did not) and for the most part I was mild-mannered enough to be left alone about it. To most of the world I was a pretty child and a quiet one. With my friends I was goofy and liked reading books and acting out Bridge to Terabithia in my backyard. I was non-confrontational and observant and then, every once in a while, explosively angry—when I was eight, I put my fist through the glass in our front door because I was frustrated my friend's little brother wouldn't leave us alone—but mostly only my family saw that side. I don't remember speaking up much, so people thought of me as intelligent, but somewhat air-headed. In high school, my older sister used to joke that I had "blond roots" and we would sing that Julie Brown song, "Cause I'm a blond, B-L-I-N-D" and I'd bounce around uncomfortably and mouth the words, pretending to be ditzy.

Being nice means catering to everyone else's needs. My father was an alcoholic, so as I grew up, I learned to pay attention to the ebbs and flows of the energy in the house. Play nice. Placate the drama. Be the strong one. Be the calm person on the boat. But it all left me feeling invisible.

I remember having the feeling that the adults in my life didn't expect much of me. To my parent's credit, they gave me a lot of freedom to listen inwardly and become myself in many ways. Well… I could be myself as long as I was *nice*. I was an unheard nice kid. The kind that teachers loved because I didn't seem to require a lot of attention.

Underneath all that niceness an anger began to boil from taking care of everyone else's needs rather than my own. At my core there was fire—the kind of fire that made a little girl punch a glass door—and it was beginning to burn deep inside of me.

Why Does a Nice Girl Try Stand-Up?

As I grew into a woman, I found myself longing for opportunities to channel that fire and to smash my way out of the Nice Girl conditioning. I was hungry to learn different ways of being a woman. My curiosity about different religions extended to different cultures, too. So I travelled the world, learning the dances of the countries and regions I visited.

I became obsessed with flamenco dance from Spain—one of the fieriest among them all!—and dedicated a couple of decades to pursuing a career as a professional flamenco dancer; but more and more the fire in me wanted to be heard, not just seen. All that hot anger gave birth to Earthquake Woman. I was burning up inside and needed to give her a voice. As I began to do so, I realized how out of practice I felt. When it came to speaking up, I felt awkward and inarticulate. Years of being nice and quiet had stunted my growth. So, I started pursuing opportunities to speak up.

All throughout my thirties and into my forties I sought out new ways to hone this voice and in doing so the Wise Woman began to emerge. I started coaching other artists and because of this I had to observe and reflect back to my clients what I saw. I became a hypnotherapist, guiding clients in and out of trance using only my voice. I started a podcast where I had to think on my feet, interview guests, and articulate my thoughts in a helpful manner. I learned to sell from the stage for my coaching practice. I gave inspirational talks at SAG/AFTRA and to groups across the country. I wrote books that involved hours of articulating my philosophies and my wisdom.

But even as satisfying as this was, there was an itch that still needed scratching. I was 42 years old and my son was in his last years of high school. My freedom as an empty nester was looming. It all left me wondering, "What is next?"

My Wise Woman was loving all the coaching and Earthquake Woman was given a place to voice her rumblings, but there was still something missing. The sense of humor, the irreverence needed a place. I needed to take bigger risks. I was a little tired of devoting myself and my Wise Woman to coaching everyone else. And then it dawned on me. I still needed to be an artist. I needed to get on stage again. I needed to pour myself back into me for a change. Little did I know this was the hormones talking.

The Queen Rescues Me from the Nice Girl

One of my good friends, Jennifer Mason, an acupuncturist turned stand-up comedian, explains it like this:

Women nurture and serve and help others for the whole first part of their lives. Then their hormones begin to change, and they don't feel like helping others as much anymore if it means sacrificing their own well-being. They become more what you might call selfish and want to put their energies inward on themselves... and you know why?" She widens her eyes and says dramatically, "Because if you don't stop giving away all of your energy you will die! You will literally exhaust yourself and have a stroke or a heart attack or whatever. Seriously! Our hormones change in part to save us from the exhaustion of serving everyone else but ourselves!

As Jennifer said this, I realized I was experiencing exactly that. Coaching and the healing arts felt like a calling for me and yet, as I entered my queen years, I began to feel more of a call to put all of that on hold in order to focus on my own art. I didn't have the energy anymore to keep a dozen creative balls in the air. It felt right to finally focus on myself. Having become a mother at 25, when had I really had time to focus on me and my own ambitions without other distractions?

The Comedian Emerges

In my early forties, I began my career as a stand-up comedian. Looking back, it's not so surprising. Growing up in the 1980s I had always loved comedy and would watch VHS tapes of Richard Pryor, Robin Williams, and Whoopi Goldberg's one-woman show, but there weren't very many famous women comics back then. In my limited experience, it didn't seem like something women did.

Then everything changed. In 2018 I watched the streaming series, *The Marvelous Mrs. Maisel*. I was intrigued and the show played a large part in increasing my willingness to try stand-up. All of a sudden, because of this fantastical and beautifully costumed show, I started to see it as something attainable for me. Watching the story of the main character, Midge Maisel, go from an angry and drunken improvised set to a determined aspiring comic, I began to see a path for myself. Representation really does matter, y'all!

From Nice to Very Naughty

On February 1st, 2019, at one of my friend's urgings, I did five minutes at an open mic. The very first joke I told on stage was the one about having sex for groceries. Before you start overthinking this idea, let me explain where it came from.

At the time, my son was in a soccer league and asking for private coaching. He mentioned a (very handsome) single dad in our community who was also a coach and pleaded with me to ask him for one-on-one coaching. Now, if you happen to have kids, you already know that, as parents, we want to give them everything. And of course this was no exception. But the idea of paying the high cost of private coaching as a single mom on top of all my normal expenses, soccer fees, school fees, groceries, Bay Area rent, and more, was unimaginable. And that's when the thought popped up: If only I could just have sex with this handsome single man for the things that my kid wants. Now that would be a win-win.

Of course, I did not actually try to bang this single dad for soccer lessons. But that one very private and scandalous thought became the seed for one of my favorite closing bits, The "Fuck for groceries" bit. The core idea being:

What if women could trade the very thing that people often want from us for those things that *we* want?

Now I get that women (and others) already do sex work, and often marriage, too, but in our American culture the clear exchange of that transaction is often kept secret or seen as shameful.

CHAPTER I - THE QUEEN YEARS

That's why it was pretty scary to say on stage for the first time, "Sometimes, I just wish that I could, like, fuck for some groceries!"

But not only did it receive the kind of shock laughter that comes from saying something scandalous, it also received the knowing laughter that comes from saying something that other people can relate to. And talk about squashing my inner Nice Girl!

Earthquake Woman thoroughly enjoyed how I ripped the fabric of society with just a few words: "Fuck for groceries!" Wise Woman nodded her head with the deeper understanding of the value of women's unvalued emotional and sexual work. And my Comedian was born!

It was the typical story of a first time doing comedy: Some things worked and a lot did not work—the two minute lecture about human trafficking I used as a set up was met with confusion—but telling everyone "I just wish it was one more way to pay. Like VISA, American Express, Discover, Venmo, PayPal, and… Pussy!" got a great response. Basically, I got enough laughs to enjoy myself and whet my appetite. Then I learned that there were open mics every night of the week. I could get up and use my voice, speak into a microphone, be heard, and do this every night if I wanted? I was sold.

As I began to do comedy night after night, the practice of it began to change me. Being present in the moment to just blurt out things off the top of my head shaped me. I took the cap off my nice-girl lid and it became hard to put it back on when I was walking amongst regular people in regular life. Or maybe I didn't want to put it back on. It felt freeing to say whatever popped into my head, to make waves, to feel my effect. It was addictive.

In the beginning it was all fun, exciting, and new. Being fresh meat, I got booked a lot as a woman before I'd even figured out my act. I even started producing some shows myself, working with the best people I could find. And eventually, the crappy side of comedy began to reveal itself: The sexism, heckling, and flat out abuse and shadiness of the scene is pretty astounding. I mean, I've lived. I wasn't exactly a spring chicken when I started and yet I have been blown away by the cutthroat and dark energy that you can find in the stand-up comedy world.

After a few years, I started to realize that mature women are not necessarily desirable on this side of show business and I realized I would have to work ten times as hard and be one-hundred times funnier to get anywhere with it. I realized all of this while my hormones were changing, my body a slowly melting wax candle version of itself, and while I was becoming even more angry at the injustices around me. Earthquake Woman was fueling me to keep going even as I sometimes wondered why I put myself through the humiliation of it all.

Being a woman in comedy is hard. We put up with all kinds of harassment: bookers who won't book us anymore because we won't entertain their advances, introductions that included comments about our "big boobies" before we take the stage, men disparaging our names with false stories, or stealing our venues just because they can, outright sexual abuse... and this is just from other comics. Then there's the heckling from the audience, the men talking over you because "they're trying to help," or the trepidatious late-night walk to the car after a show.

But as hard as comedy is, I endure it all because at the end of a night I get to stand there with a microphone in my hands. I give a voice to the life of women. However silly or trivial or crass or meaningful, I tell my stories. In a world where there are women who don't have a voice or freedoms and where they are chipping away at ours right here in the USA, doing stand-up comedy is advocacy. It's a protest gift wrapped in giggles. I open your mouths wide with laughter so that the medicine goes down easier. It's punk rock AF.

Anywhere from three to six nights a week, I stand in front of people, shaping observations into jokes, not minding my own business for once, not being a Nice Girl. I'm oversharing, cultivating a quickness, exorcizing my fury until it becomes a nice, hot, slow burn that will sustain my creativity on and off stage. I'm learning to be funny in a reliable, commanding way. I'm learning what it is like to be myself without giving a fuck. I'm learning what she sounds like. I'm learning what she moves like. I'm learning what she has to say.

Comedy Won't Make You Nice

Maybe comedy doesn't change everyone. I've met some women in comedy that seem like their skills are built over a lifetime. They sharpened their wit to a razor's edge by using it as a defense mechanism in their adolescence and now they scare me just a little bit. I was not that girl. Snapping back with words was not my go-to move—deflecting was. I was a Nice Girl, remember? And Nice Girls don't fight. They hide, freeze, or run away.

Comedy hasn't made me nice, but neither has the perimen-opausal journey. The mashup of the two has been invigorating. Neither of those things are easy journeys, but they are a rather inspiring pairing. Because here's the thing: The Nice Girl doesn't really belong up there on the stage.

I mean, she still watches (the kinky little voyeur) but she takes a back seat. Let's just say I'm out there onstage night after night horrifying my ancestors. But in my mind, I'm healing them. Venting the generational shame and releasing the built-up people pleaser in all of us, women especially.

Comedy has saved me from being trapped by the Nice Girl. It has been a rough training, but I have learned real tools of courage and commanding attention which I want to share with you—even those of you that maybe would never even dream of getting up on stage in front of people, but want to feel courageous and bold in your own life nonetheless. Within this book lies lessons from the gnarly trenches of hecklers and show business applicable to everyone needing tools to duck, dodge and forge your way through what is arguably one of the most difficult transitions of your life. These are hard won lessons from the stage that I've come to use as I step into my queen years.

So, I'm writing this book for that woman in Ukiah, who said, "My husband wouldn't let me," and for the women like her that are navigating a patriarchal system that doesn't hear us, doesn't allow us, doesn't encourage us, and definitely doesn't want us to stand up and speak our truths. I'm writing a book for women who feel dismissed, lost, and pissed off as they get older. For the women who are tired of dealing with hecklers in their lives or the guys who are "just trying to help" or capture our attention. For women who are looking for some inspiration to keep going. For women who just want to feel like someone else gets it. This book is for all of them. This book is for me. This book is for you.

But before you can own the room as the powerful provocative badass queen you were meant to be, you are required to have one very powerful currency.

The currency that everyone wants. The currency that corporations spend millions of dollars cultivating through their marketing in order to get.

You must grab their attention.

CHAPTER I - THE QUEEN YEARS

Nice Girl" in my childhood living room wearing my nicest holiday dress.

In my early forties, I began my career as a stand-up comedian.

Performing flamenco to live musicians (l to r Clara Rodriguez, Azriel "El Moreno", David McClean) Earthquake Woman is given a dance.

Dancing a piece I choreographed blending contemporary and flamenco dance (photo Taboo Media).

CHAPTER I - THE QUEEN YEARS

Explaining how to turn stage fright into magnetism to a group of actors at SAG/AFTRA headquarters in L.A.

Coaching actors at SAG/AFTRA in Los Angeles.

CHAPTER II
Attention: Playing the Fool

Have you heard of the five love languages?
Different ways that people like to give and receive love?
Like acts of service, gifts, quality time, physical touch,
words of affirmation. Well, I think there's a sixth love
language and that is playing hard to get.
Because nothing says I love you more than being ignored.

My family had a game they would play that would make me disappear. I was about three or four years old—maybe I was whining, maybe I was just existing, and someone in the family, probably my older sister, would kick it off with, "Where'd Holly go?"

My dad would pick up on the game, "I dunno. I haven't seen her! Linda!!" He called for my mom, "Have you seen Holly? We can't find her anywhere?!"

Meanwhile I'd be jumping up and down desperately. "I'm right here!!!" The idea that they couldn't see me or sense me was terrifying.

My sister would swat at the air. "Oh, I feel like there are a lot of flies flying around. Did someone leave the screen door open?"

"I'm right *here!*" I'd stomp my foot, getting more and more frustrated. I felt my breathing speed up and my face get hot.

My mom would walk in and catch on, "Oh, Holly? I don't know where she went." She'd turn and call out for me, "Holly! Holly!"

"Mommy! I am right here! I am right *here!*" My eyes would well up with tears at the idea of no one seeing me. They would chuckle and exchange smirks at my frustration. It was a seemingly innocuous little game, but it caused me pain. Deep in my little existential brain I was devastated by the idea that I had disappeared or no longer existed based on the awareness that I existed by others.

I was petrified: *If no one saw me, did I exist?*

Oh, these small moments. These small moments that shape us.

And when I look at my life through this particular lens—only feeling like I exist inside someone else's awareness, or needing to be validated by attention—my journey as a performing artist makes a lot of sense. Embarrassingly so.

But I don't think I'm alone. Every child needs and craves attention from their family.

---

at·ten·tion

/əˈten(t)SHən/

noun

1. notice taken of someone or something; the regarding of someone or something as interesting or important.
2. the action of dealing with or taking special care of someone or something.

CHAPTER II - ATTENTION: PLAYING THE FOOL

The topic of attention isn't a simple one. I should know. I'm a performer and I receive a lot of it. It always annoys me when people wave away the topic as if it's tangled with vanity, as if anyone who performs or seeks it out in any way is simply a show hog, a spotlight hugger, a boastful Betty, an overachiever diva—as if! If you think I'm here to light-heartedly joke about being an attention whore while trotting out all of my embarrassing tales, well, you're only half right. I will trot out some juicy stories, but when it comes to the topic of attention, I reserve the right to wax philosophical, dip into poetry, and let the Wise Woman speak through me. Attention is more than just a pretty red lipstick. She's the whole makeup box, the theater and the audience, too.

In exploring this topic for this book, I've identified three different ways that we relate to attention throughout our lives: as a foolish romance game, as a weapon of war, and as a method for manifestation. Since I'm about to tell you some juicy stories of naughty things I did, I think we'll start at the beginning. We'll start by trying to wrap our arms around this idea of attention and marvel at her glory....

Attention has been around for a long time, longer than humans have been here. The first moment something became aware of something else there was an energy transference. Like a match striking. The fire was lit. It has been passed around more times than a dooby at a Grateful Dead concert. And it just keeps going. It hasn't stopped. We give our attention. We receive attention. We *pay* attention. It is a currency. Attention can feel a lot like love when we want it. It can feel intrusive when we don't.

Attention exists not in one place or one time, but only in its transference. Its continuous flow from one thing or another is what defines it. If it stops flowing, it no longer exists. Or exists somewhere new, jumping around untraceable in its path. Attention is a type of currency that can flow towards people, to things, to ideas, but something about its journey from one conscious being to another makes it magnify. It flows most tangibly, most deliciously between people.

Sometimes we can feel it flowing towards us:

> *I can feel it on the back of my neck*
>
> *It tingles and I sense*
>
> *You there in it*
>
> *Even though you're across the room*
>
> *I feel you hurtling yourself*
>
> *Into me*

Attention flows between people but it also flows within us. We direct our thoughts into things. Attention is the precursor to every manifestation. Before you reach for something, there is an attention to it. Before you speak, stand, hug, touch, write, laugh there is awareness. It affects all things physical and yet it is not physical.

Especially early in life, we play games with attention, a ping pong of consciousness, as though we are somehow lacking or in need of more of it. These games with attention can play out like a clandestine romance novel. It's a satisfying read, if sometimes a tortured one. It's the steamy novel you hide under your bed because you're embarrassed to be reading it. We don't feel comfortable wanting the attention outright, but have to maneuver and dance around it in such a way as to call it towards us, our hearts fluttering in anticipation:

> *I feel your attention*
>
> *Like a knocking at my door*
>
> *I don't want you to know*

CHAPTER II - ATTENTION: PLAYING THE FOOL

That I'm home

Afraid to answer naked

And lustful

Any good romance has its ups and downs, twists and turns: the pursuit, the heat and excitement, the flirtations, the unwanted advances whilst longing for the unrequited love. We can spend a great deal of energy vying for it, flirting with it, trying to get it, and also hiding from it. Our relationship with attention when we're young can be very coquettish and filled with longing. Engaging in this kind of romance only makes us want more of it. We can become so hungry for it, we bend ourselves over backwards with different clever ways we can bargain for it:

Look here

Just loan it to me for awhile

As though the night is chilly and it's

a good scarf and you're a good friend

I'll wrap it around my neck for warmth

Take in your smell

then leave it on your doorstep

Just a little bit violated

Attention can make fools of all of us. Like when you think someone is waving at you and then you realize it's for the person behind you. We stumble over ourselves to get it and are embarrassed when we're caught doing it. Regardless of what we are doing with attention, it can't help but exist. Whether we are bargaining for a piece of someone else's, fending ourselves off from its unwanted presence, or feigning indifference to the power of our own, it must keep flowing... somewhere.

> How long can I hold
>
> This space for you without
>
> Letting someone else
>
> Flow into it?

But the game of attention changes as you go through life. Looking back on my youth I spent a good deal of time managing unwanted attention in the form of lustful glances and unwelcome advances, until one day, somewhere in my forties, all of that abruptly changed.

The Challenges of the Queen Years

You may have found that one of the challenges of this time is that people pay way less attention to you. I've seen it. People look around me instead of at me. There are less eyes that light up with excitement or turn on when I walk into a room. Attention flowing towards me has waned and in some cases ceased altogether.

It fucking pisses me off.

Grappling for the audience's attention night after night on stage has helped to ready me for this change. It has given me reason to dissect my relationship with it. Sifting back through my life and my tumultuous love affair with attention has taught me everything I need to understand about the queen years.

From the time I entered my "maiden" years—around 12 or 13 years old—I received lots of attention, often not deliberately. I was a cutie. I learned tricks. I became a sponge for attention. These were my princess years, the years I was objectified and put on a pedestal for how I looked,

CHAPTER II - ATTENTION: PLAYING THE FOOL

and in many ways served as a game piece for others to move around in their lives. I hadn't learned how to own myself yet.

And then I became a mother when I was 25. My son's father was only 27 and while I was thrilled to become a parent, he wasn't ready. He took longer to get involved and I found myself a single mother trying to make it work in the Bay Area. Every girlfriend I had back home had already started having kids, many of them single. While this didn't seem overly strange for me, it left me out of step with my peers in the Bay Area, many of whom are only now having children.

> *People in the Bay Area don't start having kids until they need reading glasses to look at the pregnancy test.*

Surviving as a young single-mom meant I had to switch gears with my relationship to attention. For the first time I became the one giving a lot of attention; nurturing, caring, and raising a young one. I loved it and poured myself into the role. But I also needed support. I had to become an emotional laborer who did both—drawing attention to me (*What a beautiful little Madonna and child! Let us give them a hand with this door!*) and also give it out to my kid in spades. I was no longer just a sponge, but a channel of energy and attention. Learning the emotional coordination required for simultaneously giving and receiving, funneling, taking it, and letting it go.

And then one day motherhood was over in the practical sense. I had my kid in my twenties, so right about the time my son was leaving the nest, my own body chemistry began to change. Just when I was feeling the desire to turn my house into a sex den and learn to waterski my body said, "Really? I don't think you're doing that." My hormones began to change and my body also said, "I can no longer go at this speed. I can no longer take care of everyone else at this intensity or I will die." My sense of survival kicked in just as the easeful energy and attention began to fade away.

It was somewhere in my early forties that the flow of attention towards me took a distinct turn. There was no real bridge for this abrupt change. Many people who identify as a woman and who are lucky enough to make it into their forties feel this. My neurochemical armor, as Dr. Mindy Pelz, a menopausal expert, likes to call it, dropped as my hormones changed and with it my energy, my ability to tolerate stress, to tolerate others.

But what happens once we are no longer young, fertile, or able to attract attention as easily?

Well, this is where we can feel lost. Everything about the way we've been operating up to this point no longer works. Any romance stories we've been playing at to get attention are no longer impactful or they take on a different tenor. All the natural attention you took for granted isn't around you in the same intensity—and this happens simultaneously as your estrogen, progesterone and sex hormones begin to leave you like it's 3:00 am and the bar is closing. You don't have to go home but you can't stay here!

Society just expects us to make this leap from our maiden selves, trained to play the romance game and vie for attention, into this all-knowing confident goddess, a self-sufficient, gracious, and wise queen... and that is a huge leap! One of the problems is we don't shine the spotlight on the queens of this world, so we aren't given very many examples of what that is supposed to look like. As young women, we grow wildly in all directions, sometimes with no idea of what we're growing towards. We can often get lost along the way working in old systems that no longer work and contorting ourselves to get our needs met.

CHAPTER II - ATTENTION: PLAYING THE FOOL

> Dr. Mindy Pelz who specializes in menopausal health calls these your neurochemical armor: "As we get older, a gradual decline in hormones, including estrogen and progesterone, leads to the subtle fade of eight critical neurochemicals that dictate things like our moods, memory, and cognitive functions. It's a symphony of change."

Contortions

When we feel disempowered in our ability to get the love and attention we need, we contort ourselves to get it. We learn who we are through our experiences with other people. Our interactions and all of our relationships reflect us back to ourselves and help shape us into adult human beings. This attention in the form of reflections can come in many forms. It's nice when it comes as love, but it can also come as criticism, cruelty, violence, and vitriol. Children who learn they can only get attention by acting up or being bad will find themselves shaped by this, becoming the black sheep just so that they receive any attention at all.

Any kind of attention is better than none at all.

I often think of something the comedian Sarah Silverman said about attention-grabbing hecklers:

> A guy once just yelled, "ME!" in the middle of my set. It was amazing. This guy's heckle actually directly equaled its heartbreaking subtext—'me!'"

Another time I was listening to Howard Stern and a young listener called in. He was being an a-hole so Howard hung up on him, but just before he was disconnected, I heard him say real quickly, "I exist!"

Both of these hecklers just wanted some kind of attention—any at all—even negative attention would suffice to feed the hunger and the need to feel seen.

One could say that attention itself is the very currency, the very driving force that shapes all of us. Sure, it's nice when it's pure unconditional love. But how often do we get that? We'll settle for bits and pieces here and there. Mangled scraps. Polluted pieces of it. Attention is that powerful.

And what if you're hungry for more of it than you can get from one person? Then you become someone who learns how to draw more of it to you. More than one person at a time. You become a performer.

Birth of a Performer

The earliest memory I have of performing I was maybe four or five years old and my dad had taken me to see a big band jazz ensemble at a mall. The twelve-piece band barely fit on the small stage in the middle of the food court. There were tables and chairs surrounding the stage with a small space, about eight feet deep, in front of the stage where someone could dance. My dad was excited. He lived for jazz music and would often pester live bands at local bars by bringing his saxophone and asking to "play in," but tonight wasn't just any old bar act. It was a special big-band.

When we arrived, he took me to stand right up front in that eight-foot space, right up close to the stage. Some members of the band smiled at me graciously and I gawked back at them and their shiny instruments. I already knew I liked music and I wiggled a little bit to imaginary music in anticipation. I was a cute little thing. With my toddler body still chubby with baby fat, my dark hair chopped into a little bowl haircut around my face, and the white collar of my dress coming all the way up to my chin, I looked like a Weeble, one of those little toys from the 1970s made by Hasbro: No neck and all face.

CHAPTER II - ATTENTION: PLAYING THE FOOL

The minute the music started, I let go of my dad's hand as the loud rhythm and melodies forced me to move. The bright sound of the trumpets was like a herald's call to some sunshine that existed in me and it was dying to be expressed. My small body started to jiggle and swerve. My feet took up steps I had only ever seen in old movies and my little legs clad in cotton tights looked like a blur as they whizzed about. I transformed into another thing entirely as I flung my head in gestures unknown to my tiny body and my face contorted in the rapture of the moment.

Pretty quickly I became the center of attention as others in the audience laughed and admired me as I allowed the music to move through me and this wonderful dance to pour out.

All I really remember was seeing the awe and joy on people's faces as they watched. I had this sensation of energy filling me as their attention did. This energy flowed through me and out to them and back to me—circular. It was so powerful it could have lifted my tiny body up off of the ground.

Afterwards, my dad was so proud as people complimented my dancing. He exclaimed, "I don't know where she learned that type of dancing! She must've just picked it up from the jazz ghosts in the room! I've never seen her do anything like it!"

My whole life I've tried to repeat some version of that experience. Cycling energy in whatever form I can with audiences, gathering the attention and giving it back. Whether it's dancing, speaking, acting, or comedy, when I do it, it feels like home.

The thing about getting a taste of this attention early was that it made me hungry for more. But I couldn't just start dancing and demand a crowd everywhere I went (though, boy, did I sometimes try!). Like most kids, I grew up with busy parents, a sister with her own needs for attention, and teachers who expected me to be nice and quiet which made it tricky to try to get the attention I craved. And when I didn't get my needs met, I sought out ways I could. Some were healthy, but as a woman growing up in the 20th century, some were not.

The Hyperventilation Maneuver

When I was in middle school I developed a hyperventilating condition. I would cry until I could barely catch my breath. This did two things for me: I got out of French class and I received a ton of attention.

I had heard about hyper-ventilating from a kid on the wrestling team named Josh. He said that he was so stressed out one time that he was unable to catch his breath, so someone made him breathe into a paper bag. It sounded wonderfully dramatic. I was already a big crier and dramatic kid who didn't receive nearly the amount of attention that I thought I required so this seemed like a great way to fill the quota. I was also a young aspiring actress at the time, still riding high from my recent role as the king in my 4H club's rendition of *Sleeping Beauty*, so as I listened to Josh describe in detail exactly what had happened when he hyperventilated, I quietly thought to myself, *I can play that*.

I integrated hyperventilating into my wheelhouse of unhealthy tools to get what I needed. Something would set me off—I missed an assignment, had to conjugate a verb, or it was just too hot in there—and I would cry, then cry harder, and then begin heaving and coughing. But the real dramatic finish came when I would widen my eyes in fear and convey with my face: "I can't breathe!" I couldn't do it too soon, but if I timed it all perfectly then the performance would gather concerned people around me. Someone would be sent to fetch a paper bag and I'd lift it to my face in relief, allowing the fetcher a moment of satisfaction in a job well done. Everyone would watch for a moment as I appeared to calm down, then they'd go back to their desks and class would resume. I would sit at my desk, a few tears of relief sliding down my face as I breathed in and out into the bag, the paper crinkling satisfyingly as it expanded and contracted, just in case anyone was trying to take their attention off of me too quickly.

To be fair, in my hormonal adolescence, I did sometimes feel a deep sadness so agonizing that it made me cry so hard I almost lost my breath. But once I found out about hyperventilating, I would push myself there. Middle-school life was moving fast. Everyone was changing and forming groups and hierarchies. Hyperventilating was one way I could slow everything down and get some sort of control over the moment, and some of that glorious attention!

Catfishing Boys at the Mall

My favorite place to hyperventilate was French class. I had thought I was going to love French. It seemed glamorous and I found French people so fashionable and chic. *Oooh la la!* Unfortunately, it was much harder than I imagined, exacerbated by the fact that my French teacher was kind of mean. But French class had its benefits and, as it turned out, helped me discover other schemes to get attention.

The best thing I got out of French class was this little act that I would do where I would pretend to be a French foreign-exchange student to pick up boys at the mall. Today, many indoor malls have become sad, empty memorials to the days before internet shopping. But when I was growing up, indoor malls were where stuff went down.

Tween-age girls were the pests of indoor malls. We weren't old enough to get one of the cool retail jobs and, having no money, we just scurried around in gaggles of twos and threes giggling, gossiping, and making our own drama.

My friends and I would often frequent the local mall to talk to cute boys. Mostly we would just stare, point, and try to get them to notice us (unsuccessfully). We faced the dilemma that many twelve-year-old girls face: Boys our age were not interested in girls yet, even though we were wildly horny for them! They weren't looking for us yet, and we rarely got up the nerve to actually approach them, but one day I had the brilliant idea that I could close this gap by pretending to be French. I mean, what good was French class if not to lure in unsuspecting cute boys? So, I memorized a French paragraph, combed my straight dark hair into a shiny neat curtain of prettiness, put on red lipstick, and topped it off with a little beret.

The scheme was simple: I would walk up to a boy and ask him in a French accent, "Eh pardon moi, do you know—ehh—what time it is?"

I loved watching their faces light up with excitement! I was the most exotic creature these little Indiana boys had ever seen! A foreign land ready to be explored.

"Where are you from?" they'd invariably ask.

"Français," I would say. "Errrrr—How you say? France."

"Wow! Really?" They'd retort. Sometimes they would demand I say something in French. And when that happened, I regaled them with my memorized paragraph. I still to this day remember the first sentence of it: "Décrivez le tour joué parle…" It was all gibberish. I didn't know what it meant then and I definitely don't know now!

It didn't matter really—they were entranced. I'd use my French name from French class, Isabel, and give them the number of my "host family" but inevitably after talking to them on the phone once or twice we'd drift off. It was too much work keeping up the ruse and to what end? They thought I was French, but I was just a girl in a beret. The most delightful part of it was the game, the chase, the initial attention.

Looking back now I realize how very little power I had. To get attention while being a Nice Girl you had to get not just good grades but be top of the class. You had to be polite and obedient in the hope that people noticed. Ugh! I was impatient and these Nice Girl ways of getting attention were exhausting!

Embarking on my little French act had opened up a new door for me, however. Everywhere I looked, from movies to TV to real life, I saw women use their sexuality for power. It seemed simple and after a few tries I discovered I was pretty good at flirting and getting noticed. And having a rather developed body at 12 years old—I looked like I was 16 when I was 12—meant that people accused me of being sexy even when I wasn't. As a result, I fell deeply into the foolish path of attention seeking and began contorting myself in order to get more of it.

The Contortionist

Trying to be a Nice Girl, exploiting the role as a temptress, hyperventilating, and pretending to be a French girl were examples of the kinds of contortions we make when we live in an imperfect world, where we feel trapped. Our needs go unmet, so we bend ourselves into all kinds of shapes to get what we think we need.

I like the imagery of a contortion because it alludes to what it does to you. It distorts you and shapes you into something that may not even vaguely resemble who you really are. It also creates angles and kinks that don't allow for the full flow of energy. Nice got me ignored, so I pretended to be sick (hyperventilated). That started to get tiring so I turned to manipulation (pretending to be French). I twisted and turned in so many directions until I was unable to sort out which parts of me were honest and which were unhealthy tactics for getting my needs met. And we all do it, these contortions. Once you see them, you can't stop seeing them. They're everywhere.

Contortionists Everywhere

One contortionist I've met a lot while doing stand-up is the helpful heckler, the guy in the audience who thinks he's helping. He has been taught his whole life that women need assistance and then he sees one on stage whom he doesn't find funny (or he just doesn't get the joke). He's also been feeling a little purposeless lately. He is not getting the attention he craves. . . . Then he sees this woman on stage and sees an opportunity to play the hero and cut a slice of the attention pie by trying to be funny in the middle of a performer's set.

These contortions can even drive our career choices. A guy grows up in a big family and doesn't get much attention except when he acts up. He becomes a comedian because that's how he knows how to get attention. But because he is so desperate to get attention, he feels unfilled, leaving him unable to be truly compassionate and empathetic in relationships. He isn't bad or wrong. He's just trying to meet his needs through a contortion.

Contortions can make us sacrifice ourselves. A young woman who has been taught that asking for what she wants makes her sassy or "difficult to work with," doesn't speak up when her boyfriend insists on unprotected sex, and then she gets pregnant. She feels trapped by her situation, but the nebulous lines of communication she's been taught as a woman prevent her from escaping.

Contortions can also turn us into monsters, shadows of the people we are meant to be, those who seek out pleasure and advance on others' space in uncomfortable ways. Our society doesn't teach us how to appropriately engage in healthy discussions about sex, so our desires become hidden. They can't really disappear (we'll talk about this in the next chapter) so they leak out in strange ways, like someone blurting out of nowhere that they really find you hot, or awkward advances, or even predatory behavior. These are just contortions in response to a world that suppresses our desires, doesn't give us healthy avenues, and leaves us all desperate for our basic human needs to be met.

As I grew up, getting unwanted attention from men made me learn how to contort to avoid their advances. I started out seeking the sweet

CHAPTER II - ATTENTION: PLAYING THE FOOL

high I got off of attention from boys or even relishing the power I had to attain second glances from men, but it felt different when I wasn't looking for it. Quickly I learned there was way more attention I didn't like: gross comments, strange advances from grown men, someone putting their arm around me, objectification. I often found myself wishing I could *just be a person*, not always a sex object. So then I'd do things to escape like ignore people talking to me, drift off and disassociate into my imagination instead of being present. But I also became so accustomed to this that I found myself rejecting and avoiding healthy and wanted advances. I became blind to them. As I still needed those things, I looked for them elsewhere: comedy, dance, performing, being overly flirty. Even though some of these things are considered healthy outlets, they can all become unhealthy contortions.

Contortions are when we have life experiences that create a bubble or blip in our direct access to getting what we want in life. Contortions are what we do instead of being loyal to ourselves, embracing our failures, being shameless, being honest, and asking for what we want.

Contortions are every single thing that happens to us when we aren't living, speaking, asking, breathing, and being in full integrity with our truest deepest desires. These contortions never become more apparent than when we begin to step into our queen years.

After You Grieve the Maiden

When my son left home for college, I couldn't have felt more ready at the time. It had been a hard couple of years keeping a teenage son cooped up during the pandemic. I was excited for him to move out into the world, make new friends, and have new experiences. I was excited to have new experiences, myself, as well.

What I didn't expect was the grief that slammed into me like a psychopathic lover I thought I'd dumped showing up on my doorstep unannounced. An empty nest subjected me to years of incredible grief I didn't see coming. The minute my son left home my mind wanted to ruminate on the past. I felt like I had been a great mother—loving, attentive, emotionally present, if busy at times. But something happened when my son finally left and I realized that part of my life was over. I thought of everything I might have done wrong or wished I had done differently and also realized I had made no plan for what the next 10 or 20 years of my life might look like. I felt all of this grief and uncertainty at a time when I was also feeling the tide of the world's attention rolling away from me....

But once I grieved this, all of these losses, there was a win that began to float to the surface.

As a woman, I spent so much of my life, from the time I was 12 until my early forties, managing other people's energy. There was so much desire coming at me that I spent a lot of time warding it off, learning ways to break the tension, to giggle, to please everyone and get out of dangerous situations still breathing. I learned how to dodge, maneuver, and dart in and around those trying to catch me so well that I didn't even have time to imagine it ending.

But it does end.

For any queen reading, even though you are stepping into a new phase of life, you are not without the memory or the skills of it all, the skills of both the maiden and the mother. You are still able to access the coquette and the nurturer if that's what you want to do. The big gift is that you are no longer forced to manage unwanted attention and you are no longer required to give it out either.

As you disappear from the world at large, you finally appear fully to yourself. For the first time, maybe ever, without having to waste your time fending people off, you are able to sit back and truly observe. Truly see what's around you. And inside of you.

CHAPTER II - ATTENTION: PLAYING THE FOOL

And when you start to look and see what is truly around you, you get angry.

And why shouldn't you?

That's when Earthquake Woman emerges.

It can be maddening and unfair and gross. *Now I have finally have so much to say and actually have the time to say it and... you find it untenable to hear it from me?! How dare you!?*

But once the anger subsides, you recognize this strange new taste in your mouth.

It's freedom.

You are free from the cycle. You exist outside of it.

You are able to reign, yet not required or beholden to the foolish games of attention seeking. You can take care of others but you are not tethered by the day-to-day tasks of mothering and care. What are you going to do now that you don't have to wipe butts and noses, fend off creeps, and spend your valuable energy pleasing everyone else?

My son is out of the house! I am over forty and I am living my best life!
This morning, I woke up, microdosed mushrooms, and went roller skating!

You've got time, queen! If you're willing to have the courage to carve your own path, the queen years can be a very lucrative, creative and empowering time.

Women are given the script that they must attract attention through the way they look rather than ask for anything directly. We are fed the archetype of the maiden (also known as the princess, the coquette, or the ingénue) who is expected to effortlessly draw attention and energy to her by fluttering her eyelashes.

So, if we don't have access to the same avenues of power as we get older, and if we are tired and done with the stickiness and self-diminishment of manipulation, then the question becomes:

How do I command attention now? If coquetry and manipulation are the maiden's tools for attention, what are the queen's?

The Opposite of a Contortion

Once we stride into our queen years, we are no longer able to maintain the contortions or play roles that others want us to. They may be literally killing us, turning into cancer, auto-immune disorders, disease, and suffering that wells up from our stored trauma. Our bodies demand that we find a way to straighten out, to bring ourselves into integrity and live in the light.

So, what is the alternative to contorting ourselves to get what we want? The opposite of a contortion is integrity. Integrity in this context is having the courage to live in full alignment with your deepest desires. You are standing by them, owning them, valuing them, speaking up for them, and not being afraid of experimenting with what all of this looks like as you figure it out again and again.

As I began doing stand-up comedy and looking back at my life for material, I started to see all of these contortions for what they were. But it begged the question: What did I really want? If I wanted to forge a new relationship with attention, one where I wasn't contorting myself to get it, then how would I do that? I had spent so much of my life catering to other people's desires, I had lost touch with what it was that I really and truly deeply desired.

If I wanted to free myself from this foolish romance story, and stop contorting myself, I had to go to the heart of why I was contorting myself. What was making me do any of it? What needs aren't being met?

I had to figure out what I desired.

CHAPTER II • ATTENTION: PLAYING THE FOOL

Madonna and child. Being a young mom meant my kid went with me to performances and rehearsals. By the time he was two he knew how to say, "Olé" at the right time in the music.

Once a clown always a clown (with my sister): my mom must have had a premonition when she made me this Halloween costume.

Trying to mimic the look of French models: 12 years old.

In my Weeble People days complete with bowl haircut (with my sister, Heather).

CHAPTER III
Desire: From Blind Ambition to Finding Your Point of View

What do I desire? I don't want to be a married woman, but I want someone to ask me and then I will say... no!

I used to think that desire was something I fabricated. I put the pieces together like a third grader who folds a piece of colored paper, puts some glue on it in the shape of a heart, and shakes glitter over it. *I made this for you!* My heart, my desires being like a particular shade of red I picked out. But what I've learned about desire, true yearning is that it is not chosen so much as stoked. You are not the author of your own desire as much as you'd like to be. We attach so heartily to our wants and passions that we think that we have something to do with them. But really, they are something that arrives inside of us. They animate us, yes, but didn't begin with us. Desires can be nurtured, beckoned, and fed; but not ignored. Once alive inside of us, they refuse to back down.

Our attention feeds them.

And also, any attempt to tamp them down or starve our desires with inattention doesn't banish them; it only makes them more like ghouls. Stripped of decorum and humanity they bang at the basement door begging to come out, surprising us in the middle of trying to host a very civilized dinner party.

Our desires, if left unattended, will haunt us.

We cannot barter with our desires to make them go away. We can only look at them dead on. Honor them. Care for them. Shepherd them into our everyday lives in such a way so that carrying them doesn't cause us crippling. Foster them so that their fruition causes no harm to ourselves or others.

There is a world where we can become partners to them as long as we don't trivialize them. Don't mistake passions for wish lists. Don't think you can intellectualize your way out of this. If you feel like you don't know what you want, it's not for lack of desire trying to be heard within you. It's for your lack of listening. Desire never left. It's more likely you've put on headphones or forgot how to turn down the noise so you can hear them.

I'm no magician of desire. I've definitely found myself off course more than once.

A few years ago, as I was first verging on my queen years, I dated someone who was the dictionary definition of a social butterfly. There was always a group around him. He was always the life of the party. For a few very exciting months I just allowed that to become my reality, too. I was going through my own struggles: I had just had knee surgery and normal life was kind of put on hold for me anyway. My mobility was compromised, I was taking a break from full time work, and there was a time when I couldn't even get around by myself or drive a car, so I just let myself be ushered around by him. As a result, I was swept up in the fun of his very social lifestyle.

CHAPTER III · DESIRE

It wasn't the first time I had done this. Growing up with my sister, Heather, just three-and-a-half years older than me, I was often globbing onto her reality and looking to her to give me an idea of what I should want. My mom put her in ballet, so I was in ballet. My sister loved books, pretty dresses, writing, and theater, so I loved all of those things, too. When we were in high school and she splashed red paint all over a white t-shirt and wrote "No blood for oil" on it to make a political statement, I made a t-shirt, too, even though I didn't fully understand the conflict to begin with. That mimetic desire kept going, too. To this day our interests overlap: I even mirrored her college degree, English, and followed her to the Bay Area from Indiana in 2001. It wasn't until I was in the Bay Area that I actually started to pursue my interests in things she couldn't care less about. She loves to roll her eyes and call me "woo woo" when I talk about psychic or spiritual stuff, among other things. The point is, eventually I managed to separate myself from her path. To locate what fit me and what didn't.

As far as the boyfriend goes, well, eventually it didn't work out (I can break up with a boyfriend, whereas my sister is stuck with me forever! *Mwah ha ha*)—I realized living his lifestyle was in opposition to my own desires—but I learned a lot about myself from that experience. Home to him meant being perpetually surrounded, always having people coming in and out and going everywhere with a group. Over the course of several months, I think we had maybe two dates where it was just the two of us.

At the other end of the spectrum, I realized that home to me was really heavy on the safety part. Home is a sanctuary where I can be fully in touch with my own desires and a space where I can write, think, collect myself, and recharge. Having too many other people around taxes my nervous system. I don't want people in my personal space all the time. I like knowing when people are coming over and I like an agreed-upon end time. I like peace and quiet. I do not generally enjoy groups. I thrive in deep one-on-one conversations. But I learned a lot from having those desires challenged.

What I was doing was something many of us get caught up in without realizing it: *mimetic desire.* It's the act of mimicking other people's desires instead of being in touch with our own genuine desires. I didn't really understand it fully until I read a great book by Luke Burgis called *Wanting: The Power of Mimetic Desire in Everyday Life.* Basically, mimetic desire happens when we want something because someone else wants it. It's something that humans often do unconsciously. You'll see this in the sold out show that just keeps selling out: *Oh! Everyone is going to that? I wanna go to that!* In high school, when you're influenced by what the cool kids are doing or the cool kids are wearing, it's all based on mimetic desire. A lot of people are making a lot of money based on making you think that other people want it. Mimetic desire is the very basis of the fear of missing out (FOMO).

Mimetic desire can manifest in unfavorable ways. For example, you think you're doing things that are fulfilling your needs in life, but if you really stop and look at it you might just be desiring things you learned as a child that no longer fit, or you're keeping up with the Joneses and copying someone else. You are steering your life based on things that aren't necessarily fulfilling your needs. They are what you assume everyone else wants.

This is one of the reasons why the queen years can be so lip-smackingly fulfilling. We become more in touch with what it is that we want and need in the first place. It can be a time of examination and refinement. We can track our desires throughout a lifetime of trials and failures, paths taken, and passions averted. Looking back at our life path not as something to punish ourselves for, but with compassion, understanding, and curiosity. It is time to poke holes in those beliefs that hold us back from pursuing our deepest desires and to become the heroes of our own stories. We are finally ready to become our own Earthquake Woman and to create the boundaries that keep us safe, sane, and grounded so that we can give our full attention to what we want, especially those creative nudges that we may or may not have had time or space to listen to before.

I allowed my social butterfly boyfriend to replace my world with his. I was trying on his sense of home to see if it could be my own and ignoring my needs for safety and security. It didn't last long, though, because one thing is for sure; the queen years can be a time when we start to feel the uncomfortableness of things that don't fit! We can no longer suffer in systems that don't work for us.

So, when I got myself out of this relationship and I looked around at my life—striving to create a performance coaching business that took up all of my time and energy—I had to be honest that I was doing that in part because I thought it was what was appropriate at my age. After my career as a dancer and choreographer abruptly ended, I doubted my artistry. I was only a year into stand-up comedy but my passion for it... I don't know how to say it other than it kind of embarrassed me. Who was I to think that I could do this? Writing jokes didn't even come easily to me! But splitting my energy between the coaching business and stand-up comedy wasn't sustainable. Ending a relationship that wasn't fulfilling my desires also helped me to become present for all my other desires. All my desires caught wind that I was finally listening and began banging on my door with their hands out. *Give me your time! Give me your attention!*

It wasn't easy to give up my coaching business. It was really inconvenient, actually. I had wheels spinning and marketing funnels built and entire books I'd written in the name of helping other artists. *"Well,"* I thought. *"I could leave them out there! So what?"* I could still allow my work to be in the world helping people without needing to be there for every second of it. If I was going to help any more artists in this world,

I needed to help this one right here. I needed to take my artistry seriously and take my inner performer down off the shelf.

Taking Things Off the Shelf

In comedy, the first joke I ever told on stage—about fucking for groceries—is still one of my favorite jokes. But it was a bit tricky to pull off at first. It's fun to shock people, yes, but oddly my long diatribe about human trafficking was not getting many laughs and made people shift in their seats uncomfortably. It was a dark topic and yet I knew there was a well of hilarity there, but I also knew I wasn't quite skilled enough to bring it out. So, I stopped telling it for a while. I ended up putting it on a metaphorical shelf. I have done this with quite a few jokes that don't quite land yet. Sometimes I'll take a break from these bits, and shelve them until I have a little bit more skill to rework them. Sometimes it's like that. You have an idea or a premise and you love it so much but you need to let it simmer, percolate, or pickle in the background.

Stepping into your queen years is like that, too. We put things on hold when we were younger, saying we will get to it when we have time. Often women return to those things they were in love with when they were younger, those things have been percolating and are ready to swell to creative fruition.

The queen years are a time to begin taking things off the shelf, or out of the closet, or hauling them up from the basement so you can look at them again. Not only desires, but also unhealed traumas you didn't have time to deal with before. The queen years are a time to clear the shit so you can finally explore underdeveloped interests and creative pursuits.

How Do I Know What I Want?

One of the biggest complaints I hear from people is that they would go after what they want if they knew what that was. So, if you're one of these people, I will provide some tools in this chapter that I use when I'm wondering the same thing. Starting by doing an inventory of what you've shelved. Sit down with a journal and answer a couple of these questions. Or have your friend interview you like you're a famous movie star. Or if you're not into this sort of thing, you can skip over this section. Do whatever you want. Isn't that what it's all about anyway?

What are Some of the Things You've Shelved?

Think back to when you were a kid, usually the years between the ages of 8 and 20 are the ripest:

What kind of activities did you do?

- What were your interests?
- What did you play? Board games, make believe, puzzles. Did you build things? Read books alone? Create a show?
- How did these activities change over time? From pre-pubescent to adolescence to young adult?
- What were you interested in that wasn't nurtured? What drew you to that in the first place?
- Was there anything that you started that you never finished? A project, an education, a relationship, an exploration of some part of yourself?
- What (if anything) were you discouraged from doing—explicitly or implicitly? Why was that—do you know? How did that make you feel?

Signs that My Soul Was Steering Me Back to Comedy

When I was grappling with my decisions about what to do with my queen years, I looked back to my childhood—the things I naturally played at and my interests—it all pointed to continuing this career as a comedian. When I was a kid, as soon as my dad purchased a camcorder, I wanted to be in front of it. I filmed countless sketches with my friends that reduced us to hysterics with every rewatch. Looking back at old home movies I was a total ham. I was the kid jumping into frame half naked as a hilarious shocking cameo. In dance class, I was constantly reinventing things to amuse myself. I'd learn the choreography the correct way and then, just for fun, I would do a little goofy version of it while I was waiting for the music to start.

The desire to be an actor was so persistent that I begged my dad to take me to Chicago (we lived in Indianapolis) to get an agent when I was 14 years old. I auditioned for movies and television and began booking things, starring in an ABC Afterschool Special when I was 16 years old. When choosing a college, I chose North Central College because of its proximity to Chicago, where I could continue auditioning for things. I would act in my college's plays and on the weekends my friends and I would take field trips to the city to watch fringe theater and see improv actors at Second City.

As adulthood took hold and I became a mother, I put my dreams of acting professionally on a shelf. I took a job as a file clerk at a law firm where they taught me bookkeeping and I eventually became their Accounting Manager. I channeled my sense of humor into life as a single mother. Being able to keep it light and laugh at life's ups and downs became my survival tool. Other dancers I knew went on tour while I took local gigs and volunteered to referee my son's soccer team. Working full time as an artist got shelved, stored for another unscheduled day. I still kept my hand in things on the side: dancing, writing, coaching, but never fully felt like I had the space to fully go for it.

Once my son went to college, all of that changed. My time was my own again and I noticed a returned energy to go out and perform every night. I found more purpose in my everyday life when I'd had that wonderful attention on stage the night before. I got more bookings on showcases and in clubs. Comedy wasn't easy, per se, but it seemed to be opening up opportunities. I was getting bigger, more prestigious gigs and getting paid more. It was still not enough to live in the Bay Area—I had to take contract accounting jobs to make things work—but by doing comedy I felt more hopeful and fulfilled in life. My ambition started to take shape.

When I was a kid doing auditions in Chicago, my ambition was blind. I didn't know what I was searching for, exactly, or what it meant to me. All I had was a feeling, a feeling that I should be performing in any way possible. And other people fed that ambition. I had a college acting teacher who wrote on a paper, "I think you have what it takes to 'make it'!" Teachers, mentors, directors, and casting directors gave me great roles, went the extra mile to help me get an audition, and just really rallied on my behalf. And here's the important part, they didn't only believe in me; they were *excited* for me. When they'd smile at me, there'd be a bit of awe and it felt like they were getting a high from just imagining where my career might go.

I believe I may have disappointed all of them… but then again, it depends on where you decide to end the story. My soul hasn't led me in a straight line but wouldn't it be a little dry if it had? Nevertheless, the energy I receive now for being an artist is different than it used to be.

When you're returning to the stage, reinventing yourself for the millionth time in your forties, not as many people support you in the same way. There's not the same excitement. It's more "Good for you" and "How brave" rather than "You know, you could really make it!" and

I personally find this infuriating. Why don't we believe in middle-aged people more? We are smarter, more prepared, more regulated, often we're more professional and have 401ks and stability. It used to infuriate me when I would get overlooked for internships, promotions, or passed at the club. Do they not think I'm serious? Like this is some kind of hobby? But then I mentioned this to another older comic. At the time, I was producing a weekly show and I was thinking of creating a residency, but only for comics over forty.

My friend, Ellis, was like, "Fuck that! That's a bad idea! You know why there aren't these opportunities for older people? Because they don't need it. Holly, you're smarter, more mature, experienced, and just better in every single way than those young kids. Own it! Take their lunch!"

I took that to heart. While I do think it would be interesting to have more opportunities for middle-aged people, I see what he means. The excitement and belief has to come from within and it starts by being honest with myself about what I really want.

When I looked honestly at the old dusty shelf, what I desired was to be an artist again. What I desired was to create, perform, and see what I could do if I poured all of those coaching resources back into myself. My soul had been on this journey a long time and they weren't giving up.

But if I was going to get on stage night after night and tell jokes, I would need to sharpen my tools. I would have to figure out what to talk about.

Getting Over Not Being Liked

(They say) one of the most important things to do as a comic is to figure out your point of view. What do you care about? What do you want to talk about and what's your opinion about it?

And my personal favorite: What makes you angry?

CHAPTER III · DESIRE

Well, there was plenty that made me angry. Earthquake Woman is a pretty loud sister. The tedium of going around saying goodbye to everyone at parties is enough to make me not want to go to parties (I'm a real big champion of the French Exit). People that pick their noses at the shared table at Peet's Coffee. Parking in San Francisco. And bigger things like men interrupting me, men discounting my opinion, men getting promoted over me for no reason other than they're men. Sexual abuse, human trafficking, the horrors enacted upon the unhoused population, kids worrying about getting shot in schools! I had anger in spades! But the Nice Girl in me clutched her pearls and wondered if people would still like me if I shared my real opinion about things. But if I wanted to actually be any good at this comedy thing, I had no choice.

"I've just accepted that there's going to be about 10% of any comedy show that I'm not going to really agree with," said a friend after years of being a fan of live stand-up comedy. She was identifying what many comedy audiences find out pretty quickly. A comedian's currency is their point of view, what they think and how they express it, how they call out the "truth" as they see it and find the humor in it that others can relate to. Or else, most others. Chances are, as with any perspective, there are going to be folks in the audience who don't agree with you, or don't like the way you express it, or just don't like you. You might hit a nerve that's too tender for them emotionally or unearth some uncomfortable truths they aren't ready to look at. Not every comic is for everyone. All of this is easy to understand when you are in the audience, but now that I was the comic on stage not being liked by everyone... a terrifying endeavor!

Finding My Voice the Hard Way

You want to find out what you stand for the hard way? Here's your task: Stand on stage and talk endlessly about things you care about. Do this unfunnily for a year or two while you figure out how to structure a joke.

Eventually, start crafting jokes. Realize that you're getting laughs but then you get bored because you stop caring about what you're talking about. Go back to the drawing board. Try to write about what you care about. Repeat the process for a few years. Then get a set together with which you can do ten, twenty, thirty minutes and get laughs repeatedly. Get bored with said material. Now, sit back and look at all of your material and dissect it to figure out what you care about and what's your point of view?

Oh yeah—don't forget to do this in front of strangers, hundreds of them. Do it so often that you get stopped at the grocery store, the gym, and other places by people who have seen you on stage. Realize you've just aired out all your most intimate thoughts and opinions to enough strangers that now you are locally famous for them. Not famous in the fun way where people are excited to talk to you and buy you drinks, but famous in a nod-of-recognition and sometimes a high five in a, "Yo, I saw you! You're so funny!" kind of way. Die small deaths of embarrassment along the way.

The good thing about starting stand-up comedy on the verge of my queen years is I do have opinions—lots of them! I have a lifetime of experiences and a solid viewpoint from which to rant and rage. Earthquake Woman was thrilled at this chance! But letting go of the Nice Girl conditioning was a nightmare at first. I would get close to saying what I wanted and back off. I would care too much what the audience thought of me (such a turnoff!). There's nothing worse than a comic who is waiting to see if you will approve of them—cringe! But *oh* how I wanted to be liked. When I first started, I would listen back to recordings or videos of my sets and it would be apparent to me straight away that my voice was thick with the need to be liked.

Another problem I would run into is writing jokes about something that I cared about and then realizing how many other comics had jokes that were too similar to mine—what I was leaning into was a trope.

CHAPTER III · DESIRE

Everyone was telling jokes like this. I needed to dig deeper and discover what I really thought. I needed to get more specific to my experience.

I started tracking my conversations with my sister and my closest girlfriends. These were the times when I let my thoughts fly, when my real opinions came out. Often, I wasn't even trying to be funny. I would simply fly off the handle and a friend would laugh and exclaim, "That's hilarious!" I would take note of it and work it into a set.

I feel like being a woman formed by this world means having to catch ourselves in the act of being a real person. If no one has asked us up to this point, or listened, or been willing to acknowledge our ideas then we can disappear to ourselves. The queen years are a good time to begin catching ourselves in the act, giving voice to fire inside, and recognizing what we stand for.

If we are to move forward shamelessly, truthfully, persistently asking, we'd better know for what. We'd better feel like we have the substance to back it up.

Not Being Liked is a Gift to All!

As I gained more skill at figuring out what I stood for and accepting that not every comic is for everyone I began to see this not as an unfortunate fact, but actually a bonus. An education in the way someone else thinks. An empathy development tool. *My dick jokes aren't just crass; they're a gift to all!*

Think of it this way: When was the last time you listened to a perspective you didn't agree with—all the way through? Tell me about a recent time you had to sit and listen to something without the option to flip the channel, block it, unfollow it, or simply scroll past it? Unless you are actively seeking out live theatre, arts, or other media, I bet your answer is *hardly ever.*

Our virtual lives are a buffet of options and experiences carefully curated by likes and algorithms that determine what we might find interesting or relevant. Live stand-up comedy is the antidote for this. Live comedy has tremendous value because beyond just making us laugh it also forces us to listen. On any one showcase you hear from a variety of different points of view sharing their truths or the funny parts of life as the way they see them.

We forget how powerful that is.

We forget how much we need it.

Stand-up comedy can build tolerance muscles.

Self-Knowledge as a Weapon

Okay then, so I am a warrior of empathy! Goddess of Awkward Silences! Out here sharing my singular perspective and making you listen whether you like it or not!

Wait... That doesn't seem quite right either.

At first when I was finding my point of view, the work I'd do in open mics could feel like that. *I have an opinion! And I'm jamming it down your throat! I am Woman! Hear me roar!*

But after a while, I began to notice I wasn't getting laughs from regular people who were not comics. Other comedians will laugh at all kinds of dark, twisted, and dumb things because we've become ground down by the heavy edges of a billion bad jokes; but, getting laughs from folks whose souls are actually fully intact takes another level of finesse.

Having a perspective didn't just mean telling people my opinion. It also required a level of craft and most importantly self-awareness. Also, I couldn't make everyone else the butt of my jokes, I had to find the humor in my own self-righteousness, my own awkward human stuff. I

CHAPTER III · DESIRE

had to know who I was and even more importantly, I had to know how the audience saw *me*.

As a comedian and as a queen, knowing who we are becomes a superpower. We weaponize our own ability to see ourselves honestly.

One of the few benefits of starting stand-up comedy in my forties was that I already knew who I was to some degree. I have a pretty good sense of what I'm about, my values, what matters to me, what I want to talk about.... Making those things funny is another thing entirely, but at least I came into it with a point of view and a sense of how the world saw me.

One of my favorite opening jokes:

My son is twenty-two years old now... [long pause] All right, usually people are more surprised by that. Fuck you guys!

It always gets one of the biggest laughs because the audience immediately recognizes me as a woman who thinks she looks younger than she does. What began as an offhanded truthful spontaneous comment has become part of my set because it gets such a good response. I am letting the audience know that I understand how they see me and making myself and my vanity the butt of the joke. Understanding how I'm viewed from the outside helps me crack jokes that will immediately get a laugh. Making fun of myself helps the audience relax and be a little more on my side.

There was a period of time when I was flirting with the idea of doing roast-battle comedy. In a roast battle, two comedians spar with creative mean jokes about each other. I had judged a couple of contests which is the ideal position to be in. The judges at roast battles mostly just make funny comments and roast the roasters throughout the show—they don't typically get roasted themselves; but I was considering actually trying my hand at battling. By hearing how other comics roasted me, I would get an honest view of how people really saw me. I'd be able to borrow some of those perspectives to work into my own comedy. I was afraid, though. Would I get my feelings hurt? I was explaining my hesitation to my friend, Morgan, who won the Grand Championship in roast battling at South by Southwest one year, and she jumped in immediately to correct me, "No, you won't get your feelings hurt. You know why? Women are so much harsher to ourselves in our own minds than any of these dude comedians could ever be. So, in a roast, we're resilient AF. But these dudes? They can't take it. You should see it. You roast them then watch the light die in their eyes." She smiled with satisfaction and her eyes went misty. "It's beautiful."

In comedy, being able to handle hearing mean but truthful things about yourself can be a real strength because understanding how other people see you is capital. It becomes a weapon. A resource. In our queen years this is something we get to have fun with as well. Our self-awareness becomes not only part of our charm, but something that influences how we craft our lives.

So I became more okay with sharing my truth, as I realized how important it was. I became more okay knowing I might be disliked. As Earthquake Woman raged, my Nice Girl sat in the darkened theatre horrified but also—I'd like to think—liberated.

The Anatomy of Courage

When I tell people that I'm a stand-up comedian, 90% of the time people say, "Wow! I could never do that! That seems very brave!"

One of the sneaky things that stand-up comedy does for the people watching it is the transference of courage. We love to watch people doing things we won't do because it makes us feel like maybe we can borrow a bit of that courage. It's why I can't get enough of watching Simone Biles doing gymnastics in the 2024 Olympics, or why my son is obsessed with the NBA, or why some people love watching videos of extreme sports. We

CHAPTER III - DESIRE

may never do that thing ourselves, but just by watching someone else do it, we leave a little braver and a little more inspired than we were before.

I've gotten up on stage thousands of times now and it does get easier and easier as I go. It's as though I've practiced and built up certain muscles that help me execute the moves. And whenever I take a break or haven't been up on stage in a while, I feel it. In this way, I've come to recognize courage as a set of muscles that I need to keep using or they'll atrophy.

These invisible muscles are:

1. Boldness
2. Persistence
3. Shamelessness
4. Honesty
5. Loyalty

Here's what's neat about them: These five different muscle groups of stand-up comedy courage are the same as those that helped me step into my queen years. It is because of these five muscles that I climbed my way out of the dark tunnel of hopelessness that can be perimenopause. It is because of these five muscles that I'm able to withstand the hecklers in comedy and life.

So, for me, as I stood facing the great unknown of my queen years, attention towards me waning, my heart longing to be on stage and in front of people, not only did I need to get in touch with my perspective, but I needed to find the courage to voice it. And I needed to go big! I needed to be bold!

I had to do the one thing that all nice little girls had been trained out of since before they can remember. In fact, we've been conditioned so deeply not to do this one thing that we will often suffer in silence.

We would rather agonize for hours strategizing how to manipulate a situation to get our desires or our needs met than to do this one thing.

I realized in horror that this one thing was finally coming for me.

I couldn't avoid it any longer.

If I wanted to follow my dream I was going to need to start *asking*.

CHAPTER III - DESIRE

I've always been enthusiastic about cake: 1 year old with my sister, Heather.

A young actor in Chicago: 15 years old and checking out the Willis (formerly Sears) tower with my dad after an audition.

My first acting headshot was taken by my dad: 14 years old.

With my theatre friends playing one of the Pigeon sisters in the "The Odd Couple" my sophomore year of high school. At my left, Elizabeth Marie Janes and Mark Charles Meyer.

CHAPTER III - DESIRE

In my forties at open mics finding my voice night after night.

CHAPTER IV
Boldness: Asking for the Gig

You know why women have a hard time asking for what they want? Santa Claus. Little girls are taught that in order to ask for what you want you have to sit on a strange old man's lap and whisper it into his ear. Gross.

I heard a comment once that made my mouth drop open in horror, though it didn't actually surprise me: Every little girl, by the time she is only five years old, has learned that she has to get what she wants without asking for it.

As someone who has booked and produced a lot of comedy shows I can tell you the number of women comedians who pop into my DMs to ask me for a spot on a show doesn't even begin to come anywhere near the number of men who do it. Over a five-year span, I can count the women who have asked me for a spot on one hand. Compare that to the *hundreds* of men who have rolled into my DMs and demanded to know *when* I will book them. It is true that there are fewer women in comedy, so they may not need to ask as often, due to a higher demand. But for the most part, I don't hear from women simply because we are conditioned not to ask. Instead, we are taught to wait patiently to be asked. We are told: *Don't be brazen. Don't be demanding. Don't be bossy. Don't ask.*

Opening our mouths and asking for what we want goes against the way we've been socially conditioned (there's that Nice Girl again). When we do ask, we often get the feedback from the world that this kind of direct activity is not "ladylike." It's too pushy somehow. We get the message from a very early age that if we want something we will need to maneuver, lie, and manipulate in order to get it without seeming like we wanted it in the first place.

Maddening!

This is crazy making patriarchal training at its very best.

Understanding how deep this conditioning goes makes it a little easier to give ourselves grace for having a hard time asking. When I tell women from the stage that they should just *ask for what you want* more often than not I see the silent response in their faces: *It isn't that easy, Holly.*

I totally get it, bestie.

Ask for What You Want is printed on some of my merch. It's meant to be encouragement. A reminder to be bold, to buck against our conditioning as women and to speak up and ask. But when I started using it, I don't know if I fully realized how confronting that request might appear to some people.

There are not one, but two words that can spark terror in women's hearts in that sentence: *ask* and *want*.

While asking for things can seem a ridiculous reach for us at times, it doesn't even speak to the terror that is desire. To want something? Pffttt! Most of us have been so cut off from what we desire that it takes all the breathing and journaling and weekend women's workshops "getting in touch with our spirit" to even come close. I'm here to remind you that this

CHAPTER IV · BOLDNESS

isn't normal, this cutting off from our desires. It shouldn't be that hard. And yet here we are so mournfully trained away from even beginning to listen to our desires that it can take hours of retraining to even begin to know. In some ways we have had so much shame conditioned into us by even having them that we've buried the truth of them deep inside us where they're difficult to identify.

Here's the fun invite I have for you though: Play around with asking. Maybe even do it before you know fully what you want. I don't think not knowing yet should hold you back from exploring. We often think we need to understand it perfectly and have every step figured out and foolproof before we even begin asking. This is not so.

You may not even be fully present to everything you want but the only way you're going to know is to start asking. Before you ask, the desire swims around in muddied waters and you can hardly make out the shape of this thing inside of you: it splashes, it backflips, you can feel it but have no idea what's really causing the commotion. You have to try to catch it, to take it out and hold it up like a proud man in a dating profile picture to really see it and begin to get a sense of whether or not you are even fishing in the right pond. Asking for what you desire and getting what you desire is an experimental process. That's why consent is a moment-by-moment process of permission. You can ask for one thing and then discover it doesn't quite satisfy the way you thought, thus opening up the opportunity for greater refinement.

The sooner you start asking, the sooner you start exploring, the sooner you'll begin to really get to the bottom of what you want.

Asking for the Gig

"Hey, I heard you are running a great showcase at ye olde brewery. I'd love the opportunity to get on it sometime. Can you keep me in mind?" is a request I've dropped into bookers DMs many times over.

What I like about this approach is I'm keeping it succinct. Bookers don't always have time or care to indulge in a chit chat and definitely don't want to hear your whole inner process leading up to this part where you reach out to them. And yet, in that brevity I also manage to compliment them on their "great show," tell them I'd love to do it and then directly ask them a question, "Can you keep me in mind?" Too often in the past I have given in to the nice-girl conditioning to drop the idea in front of them like a handkerchief and just hope they'll pick it up, saying something like, "I'd love the opportunity to get on it sometime…" But I've had much more success by ending with a question mark. People feel a bit more beholden to answer when there is a question mark. A question mark is a call to action: Reply now!

Now I can tell you, I don't always get a response. Sometimes bookers, who are other comics I see all the time in the scene at other shows, will just completely ghost me. Sometimes I have to ask multiple times. Sometimes they never answer. Sometimes they say no. Sometimes give me a "Maybe someday." But I've noticed my bookings on months where I do ask and months where I don't and I always have more when I do reach outs like this one above. The idea that you miss out on 100% of the gigs you don't ask for is a piece of wisdom I repeatedly remind myself of.

When Existing Feels Like Asking

> *The Comedian says, "You can dominate the audience by asking them something. Put them on the spot. Make 'em talk. Like a cop. They probably won't say anything funny, but neither are you and it's time to make something happen."*

Even just being on stage as a comic is a lesson in asking because I'm asking for attention again and again, night after night. In the beginning of doing stand-up, I would feel a bit of what you might call a visibility hangover after shows. Even if they were good shows, I would feel the high of having a great show. But then anxiety would creep in. At first, I just identified it as some kind of after effect of stage fright, but I think it's more than that. When you do something new, or put yourself out there in the world, you force yourself to expand. You are taking over a greater space and this can feel disorienting. It takes a while to grow yourself into that new expansion.

This can be true for adventures other than comedy, including launching your new business, taking a new leadership role within a group, speaking up at a meeting when you don't normally, or posting something on social media. If it feels bigger for you than you are used to then it can come with a vulnerability hangover. *I can't believe I just asked for that much attention from people.*

Asking and attention go arm in arm. In a way, just the very act of asking for what you want is also asking for attention. So just like with attention, when it comes to asking, we want to get what we want, but we freeze under the spotlight. (Anybody else ever have a lover ask you directly what you want and you come up stammering and shy?)

This kind of desire for attention and then a shrinking from it is a contortion, a game of hide and seek that many of us play.

Hiding and Seeking Attention

When I was a little kid there was nothing more thrilling than a game of hide and seek. I'd dream up where would be the cleverest place to squeeze my tiny body away from the seeker while someone else counted down and the anticipation built. I'd hear footsteps advancing and retreating as they'd search and search and I'd snicker inwardly at their inability to find me. I loved that thrill of someone looking for—seeking me out, their breath heavy and loud as they'd get closer. Next, it's my turn to outsmart the one hiding. Not only would I try to find them fast, I'd be nonchalant about it. "That was too easy, I can see your sleeve sticking out from behind the couch."

Hide and seek is one of the very first games that we play as children—even peek-a-boo is like an infant version of this—and it is played in every culture around the world and my very lazy Google search tells me that it dates back to at least the second-century B.C. in Greece. This thrilling game of attention is ancient. It's so ubiquitous because it hits our primal need to protect ourselves and hide and also to hunt.

Remember when you were a kid playing hide and seek? Did you ever get tired of hiding when it was taking too long to be found? You would cough or make a fart noise just to grab their attention. You were hiding away but you also loved that someone was looking for you. You didn't want to lose their interest.

I feel like this game parallels so much of a woman's relationship with the space she takes up. Our entire lives are spent either seeking attention or shrinking from it. I suppose there are a blessed few who barely think about attention, its presence or absence, and take it for granted as though it were sunshine and they were kittens warming themselves in it forever. Good for you. But for the rest of us, we are usually either desperately trying to get attention or shuddering from the burn of its gaze.

If you're anything like me, you alternate between both.

My entire life has been a game of hide and go seek. Desperately wanting attention, receiving the wrong kind and then hiding. I seek and hide, hide and seek. From the time I can remember, I've been falling over myself to get attention and also learning how to disappear.

The Booker Who Didn't Like "No"

> *My son loves the game of hide and seek, but one day I'll teach him hide and regret. It's where you hide from life and regret every decision you've made.*

CHAPTER IV · BOLDNESS

This particular booker and I had a pretty good rapport. I had performed at his venue several times and was one of his regulars. He would reach out to me. I didn't even have to ask. He was one of the first bookers who started booking me regularly, who told me I was hilarious. I considered him one of my champions.

Until the day he slid into my DMs.

I had posted a silly story that day about what the most ideal day would look like: *Writing, hiking amongst the trees, cooking something nice, oh and sex in the afternoon thank you very much!*

He responded to this with a private message. "I'll have to ask my wife, but my afternoon is free."

Ew! I was not only grossed out but I was deeply disappointed. Here was a relationship that I had thought was all above board. I was talented and he wanted talented people performing at his venue. Suddenly, his flippant suggestion threw all of this into question for me. Had he been waiting for this chance all along? Did he even think I was talented in the first place?

I grappled with how to respond. Did I say nothing and invite more advances like this? Or say something and risk offending him? I hemmed and hawed and finally decided we had a good enough rapport to survive some direct communication. I didn't like what he had said. I didn't want more of it, so I was going to ask for what I wanted.

A day later I wrote back:

> Hey, I know you were probably just kidding, [the Nice Girl in me had to make an appearance and let him off the hook] but that comment made me really uncomfortable. As someone who books me, you are effectively my employer and have some power over my career and so I would prefer it if you didn't say things like this. Thanks!

He immediately deleted his original message and stopped corresponding with me altogether. I wasn't booked for an entire year after that.

Hiding and Seeking—You get the attention and then have to grapple with the icky situations that come with it.

And that's the thing about asking. That's what makes it so tough. We don't always get what we want when we ask. Sometimes asking makes us want to hide and regret ever opening our mouths. So as I grapple with these messy situations I feel like crawling under a rock. But then I hear Wise Woman's call:

> It isn't what happens to you in life, it's how you deal with it. Life can train you to shrink if you let it or it can teach you to be courageous.

I refuse to let the creeps train me. I choose to be courageous!

I did speak up and he did retaliate, but he wasn't my only avenue for doing comedy. He was just in charge of one venue. I focused on the other places that did want me there. I ranted about it to my sister, outraged. I worked through it in therapy sessions. I kept going. About a year later, he announced his venue was closing and in a weird way I felt like I had won. In the end, he gave up. I didn't.

Asking When It's Hard

Asking is the bridge between my desires and your boundaries. One of the things that makes us hesitant to ask is that it doesn't feel great to have a wish or request that isn't granted or fulfilled. Your desires may overstep what someone else is comfortable with, so there is a feeling of friction when our needs or wants bump up against another person's boundaries, needs, or wants. Brené Brown has an idea she introduced in her book, *Rising Strong*, called "rumbling" which is, in part, when you decide to have a conversation even though it isn't easy, such as staying in

CHAPTER IV · BOLDNESS

a relationship and being willing to have vulnerable conversations even when they're difficult.

When things get uncomfortable or when our asks are met with a "No," many of us retreat, shrink, or contort ourselves to avoid conflict or stop wanting the things we want. But suppressing your desires can make them leak out in unhealthy ways. A better path is to see this point of friction as an area for growth and opportunity.

I was in a workshop recently and a great facilitator gave me this nugget of wisdom that is derivative of the work of Human Awareness Institute founder, Stan Dale:[2]

Ask for 100% of what you want

Be prepared or open to a "No."

Stay in the relationship until it is a win-win.

I like this model so much and have had so much success with this simple framework that I have begun using it every time I have an ask that feels daunting or scary. Let's dissect why it is such an effective model. How about that first line? *"Ask for 100% of what you want."*

What I want you to hear most is the 100%. Not 50%, not 80%, but the full 100% of what it is that you want. This is important because how often do we hedge and only ask for a little piece of what we want and then feel deflated by the results? You deeply crave an entire weekend to yourself to work on that creative project but figure that's never gonna happen so you ask for an afternoon. You really wish your family could take a vacation for the holidays this year instead of piling into your house where you

---

[2] Human Awareness Institute or HAI Global is a 50+ year old non-profit organization dedicated to creating a world of love and acceptance promoting personal growth and social change mostly through workshops and retreats. To learn more visit hai.org.

end up doing the majority of the entertaining, cooking, and cleaning, but you don't think anyone's gonna go for it, so you ask if you can all go out for dinner on Christmas Eve. You want your lover to talk dirty to you, but you're afraid to ask directly so you ask them to "get into it more" in the bedroom. Not wanting to appear too greedy, needy, or wanting, we will ask for less. Often this leaves us not only unsatisfied, but also more frustrated than when we started.

Often, we get to what we want by being honest with ourselves about what that really is. When people ask for less than 100%, it could be because they're unclear about or even unwilling to see that full desire in themselves.

Like I mentioned before, many times we have an idea of what we want that we can only explore through asking, so if we start with a clearer ask to begin with, going for the full 100% of what we *think* we want right off the bat, then we are much more likely to avoid confusion and get to down to the heart of the need and what's satisfying to us much sooner.

Now what about that second line? *Be prepared or open to a "No."*

Learning to say no can be difficult at times but so is hearing it. It can feel like rejection. We have a tendency to take it personally. It can feel like while someone is saying no to our request that, really, they are saying "No" to us as a person. Learning to take a "no" is a hugely important skill that few of us practice, in part, because everyone is playing nicey-nice and agreeing to things that they don't want and things they have no business agreeing to in the first place. People won't tell you "No" as much as they should in favor of doing one of the following: flaking, ghosting, standing you up, being irritable in hope you'll just get it, being outright mean, passive aggression, talking about you behind your back, and the list goes on and on.

As a culture, we deeply fear THE BIG NO. We will do almost anything to avoid saying it. And yet there is so much freedom and deeper trust to develop in our relationships if we work on it. I think about my friends who have done personal growth workshops, who have done the deep work on themselves, and how comfortable I am asking them for things. I'm comfortable because I know they will take care of themselves and say "no" if they need to. And I trust that they will say it with love and kindness because they truly want to be there for me when they can. These are the friends I reach out to because they know their personal boundaries. But if we are going to feel comfortable asking people for things then we also have to get comfortable accepting a "no."

And finally, let's dissect that last sentence: *Stay in the relationship until the outcome is a win-win.*

You aren't dropping the ball. You aren't retreating. You are staying present to the thing in between you (the asker and the asked) even when it feels like conflict—*especially* when it feels like conflict. You pay even more attention to it. You question it. You feel it out. You look for where it wants to go. You look for the next transition.

It's this last piece of advice—stay in the relationship until the outcome is a win-win—where I have some reservations. I think sometimes you can do this and when you can preserve the relationship, you should. But then there are times that you just can't.

Boundaries and Saying "No"

I remember the day I realized I wasn't going into business with a guy.

I had a conversation with a friend whom I was considering going into business with. I had started noticing a pattern where we would have lengthy phone conversations during which I would let down my guard and reveal what I was really feeling, then later he would twist what I had said and weaponize it. He used those intimate confidences I had shared against me.

Earthquake Woman rumbles, *"Anyone who will use your willingness to be honest and vulnerable against you is a huge red flag!"*

On this particular day, I felt like the pattern was cemented. I was calling him from the road and updating him on a prospective venue to produce shows. I fell into the "trap" with him of being honest about how I really felt. I revealed that my deepest concern was that a certain venue didn't want to work with me because I was a woman. We talked about that and then moved on to some other things.

Later as we were about to end the conversation he casually mentioned, "I'm going to be in the Bay this week. I think I might just need to go visit that venue and talk to this owner myself."

Hang on.... wait. What? Earthquake Woman rumbled again. A fine line of hot lava seeps up my esophagus and oozes slowly out of my mouth.

"Hang on a second," I said carefully. "You are stating—not asking but stating—that you are going to go to the venue. This is my deal that I've been working on for months. Why would you do that?"

He replied, "Well, you said that you thought he was discriminating against you because you're a woman. What you really should have done was you should have had me at that initial meeting."

"See that?" Earthquake Woman asked. *"See how willing he is to blame and fault me in this scenario? Let's eat him for lunch!"*

Wise Woman responded, *"How about we just ask him a question instead?"*

"What are you trying to do?" I asked him pointedly.

He seemed impervious to my irritation. "I figure *I* can go there and make him love me like I always do. People always love me. And then I can get that venue."

Earthquake Woman retorted, *"The hell you will!"*

The Comedian chimed in, *"Check out the hero on this guy! Wow, coming to save the day, are ya, buddy?"*

CHAPTER IV · BOLDNESS

And then the Wise Woman spoke again, *"Just ask. Ask for what you want. But let him know it's not a question."*

"I didn't ask for you to do that," I told him firmly. "Please don't go there without me."

He sneered at my boundary. "Well, fine," he said. "You see, you have trust issues. You don't trust me, just like he doesn't trust you. You are propagating the same energy as he is. That's probably why he won't work with you."

Earthquake Woman promptly erupted, *"WOW! Not only blaming me again, but adding a whopping dose of gaslighting!"*

I took a deep breath and named what was happening. "I don't like this," I said. "I am feeling manipulated by this conversation and I don't appreciate it."

The Wise Woman breathed, "Well done."

"I don't want you to go there without me," I said again, "and I don't like the way you are using what I said in a vulnerable confession to you against me in this conversation."

Now if he had simply asked me if I wanted him to get involved then that conversation could have gone an entirely different way. He would have given me, the owner of this project, the choice and I could have considered the benefits and either chosen to have him be involved or not. But instead, the way he approached came off like a threat.

The thing about asking is once you start learning to do it yourself, you begin noticing when others don't. You are more aware of the manipulation and brute force at play.

Why did he want to get involved to begin with, whether I wanted him to or not? I'll never know, but trying to make me feel bad for not liking that tactic was confusing and manipulative. So I cut through that cloudy knot with the knife of truth. This is what's happening. This is how it is making me feel. I don't like it and here is my ask.

After the call, Wise Woman whispered, *"Walk away when you must. Walk the goddess walk."*

I have not bothered to follow up with this person since.

Now if I had allowed his manipulation to play out, allowed myself to take on the attributes he was gaslighting me with, the Nice Girl in me would have been happy. *Let's make nice. Agree. Be peaceful.* But by appeasing the inner Nice Girl I'd be putting myself in danger. This is why boundaries, learning them and using them in our queen years becomes so vitally important.

As important as it is to know what it is you desire, it is also important to know what you don't want. What are your boundaries? What are you willing to put up with and what's not acceptable? These are things that you are learning in your twenties and thirties which is part of what can make those years so challenging.

It's much harder to erect a fence after a neighbor's gotten used to crossing into your yard. It's much easier to establish boundaries in the beginning. So, we fumble along, sometimes learning what doesn't work for us after it has pushed our buttons, not yet recognizing the patterns. We have less intuition because we haven't encountered as much at this earlier age. In our twenties and thirties, we are in the middle of creating our story. We are living it often unconsciously. We can only recognize a pattern in hindsight. And those young years are when we are living out of beliefs that we may have adopted and never examined.

As much as it is important to foster your point of view and become present to what you believe in, you also define what you don't believe in. Where are your edges? What do you say no to? Sometimes we become most present to our desires, to the edges of the psychic property that we inhabit, when someone challenges them. Or tries to climb the fence. There are tons of people who will push your boundaries in show business and the world of stand-up comedy is one of the worst: asking if you're available to perform but then it's like pulling teeth to get all of the details of how much you're going to get paid; bookers who will give you opportunities but then hold it over your head for favors; asking you to come to the gig at a certain time but then making you wait as they delay the show and delay and delay.... Any time you have a business where people are hungry for stage time, there will be people there to exploit that hunger and cross boundaries to do it. Early on in comedy I met many people daring enough to attack my fortress. Little did they know I had it pretty well guarded.

Integrity: Supple Asking

What about times when asking works out well? One clear example comes to mind:

My friends Kellita and Joyful joined me at the Banya, a San Francisco spa filled with hot tubs and saunas. We were having a day of relaxation and feminine bonding. Kellita is a performer and teacher who weaves together burlesque performance with an astute understanding of psyche and psychology and a deep respect for soul. Joyful is also a solo story performer as well as a story midwife to countless students. They're both total Wise Women.

It was the Winter Solstice, so not only were we soaking in the waters, we were also soaking in the wisdom and stories of each other. At one point, we were all three in the steam room and Kellita had felt like she'd had enough and was ready to leave. Perched on the top step, she called out graciously to a young man standing in the middle of the room. "You there, sir, do you mind giving me a hand down from here?" He jumped at the chance to do it, moved closer to her, and carefully helped her down from the slippery ledge." Later, as we were eating a gorgeous Persian meal together deep in the heart of the Mission District of San Francisco, I reflected on how gracefully Kellita had asked for something.

"I loved the way you asked him, Kellita," I said. "It felt so... well... queenly. Expectant that he would help, but not demanding. It was just... great."

She responded, "Yes, that feels like a beautiful place to be. I like that state of, *I am open to receiving your assistance, collaboration, and support and I am clear of how that would be.* That's lovely. It's clean receptivity. There's no guilt trip, martyrdom, manipulation. There's no collapsing, or *you need to help me*. It felt clean and supple."

"Supple?" I asked, eager to dig deeper.

"I don't know how else to put it," she said. "Supple. Supple can go for sexy but also just being open to receiving. It's also resilient."

So how do we get there, aside from spending the countless hours that Kellita has in the laboratory with her burlesque business? How do we create our own miniature laboratories for learning how to become better, more supple askers and receivers? I've got at least one idea. And it's a situation that comes up quite often.

And Then the Bill Comes: A Laboratory in Asking and Receiving

Don't you just hate it when you're out to dinner with someone new and the bill comes... and you haven't figured out yet which one of you doesn't have maxed out credit cards? The bill comes and you find yourself locked in an awkward staring contest. On the surface you wear warm smiles and maybe murmur, "Well, this was nice," but underneath there's tension. Maybe one of you excuses yourself to the bathroom, silently hoping the other person will take care of it, or you launch into a story hoping to postpone the awkward exchange. The bill just sits there on the edge of the table, like a fart in the air you're trying to ignore.

The bill in this situation is the symbol for the ask itself. It's asking to be paid. It's a situation that needs resolution. The ball is in the air, two

CHAPTER IV - BOLDNESS

people are next to it, and it's unclear who will open their arms for it and who will step back and surrender.

How do you handle these types of situations? Do you let it sit there until the other person can no longer hold the tension and rescues everyone by whipping out their wallet? Or are you the one who breaks the tension, saying, "So you wanna split this?" Or do you rush in and play the hero with a cavalier, "I've got this."

Depending on the situation and the dynamic, I've played all of these roles or one of my craftier ones where I've been known to ask, "Would you like me to help *you* with that?" Letting the person know that I'm assuming it's their responsibility, and giving them the opportunity to feel generous by saying, "Oh no, thanks. I've got this!"

The bill coming is a delicate dance that is a great laboratory for getting comfortable with asking, receiving, allowing, and holding tension. There is no one way to handle it. I'm not here like a modern-day Miss Manners to tell you how to handle these things, but rather I would like to invite you to simply use these moments as a barometer for where you are on the scale of receiving and giving. You are welcome to try out Stan Dale's guide for asking:

Ask for 100% of what you want.

This could be a variety of things depending on how you feel with that person at that moment. Here's a wide range of options:

Will you allow me to pay for this?

I'd love to split this with you…

Do you mind paying the bill?

Be prepared for a "no." Some things you should be prepared to hear:

No, I would prefer to pay.

No, I don't feel comfortable with that.

No, I am not in a position to do that.

And then stay in the conversation until it feels like a win for everyone. If you asked them to pay and they balked at the idea, instead of shrinking or feeling embarrassed about it, how about you choose something else? You could ask a question, state a need, or offer an alternative:

"I've only got ten bucks, could you cover the rest and I can pay you back on Venmo?" (Notice how this is clear and honest about exactly what you need.)

If they don't want you to pay and this makes you uncomfortable, instead of sitting silently with that feeling, try using it as an opening for connection and curiosity.

You are so generous! Thank you. I do feel a little vulnerable having you pay for everything, though. I just wonder if there is some expectation that comes with that?

Or you don't have to do any of these things if you're not ready to start asking. Just bringing awareness to the experience can be enough to start changing your relationship with asks.

Next time you're out to eat with someone and the bill comes notice how it makes you feel. What is your first instinct? What are the moves that you make or don't make? What ends up happening?

In examining moments like this, where there is an ask out there, you can begin to unwrap where you are with your own asking process. How much of your response is owed to your upbringing, your culture, your conditioning? Does this bleed over to how you deal with other asks in your life? How much of your response is related to your self-worth? And finally, are these moments easy for you or do you have a lot of emotional charge around them? Either way, what do they reveal about you and what you believe about yourself? Is there anything you would like to change about how you respond?

The Contortion

You may try and ask for what you want, but then it feels scary. You feel like you showed up to the party with no pants on. You can't bear the silence or the space between asking and finding out the answer. It's so unbearable you might even rush to cover it up, take it back, delete the text. You tell them never mind. Never mind. You apologize for it. Or diminish it with something like, "Or if not, it's okay." You feel disgusted when you do this. You beat yourself up for asking in the first place and try to shut down that desire and convince yourself you don't need it after all. Or maybe you ask for some of what you want, but not all of it, and you hope the other person will guess the rest. It gets to the point where now when you open your mouth to ask for something it has become so loaded with your assumptions that you won't get it that you sabotage the entire exchange. It feels awkward to everyone involved. So, you start to shrink into yourself. You get angry or irritable when you see other people asking easily. Or you go silent. You skulk off. You vow to never ask for anything ever again. You know this is ridiculous. Intellectually you get that it's okay to have needs, but your body tells you it would rather turn into compost. You've forgotten how to ask without a charge because you can't remember what it is like to receive.

The Comedian Tells a Story: If Vomiting Sufi Guy Can Do It So Can You

Gross-out warning! This story should not be consumed in conjunction with a meal, your cheese, your chocolate, your snack, or your second breakfast. Put down your fistful of pasta. It is a good story. It's worth it.

Many years ago, when I was visiting Egypt, I went to this mosque for a performance of Sufi whirling. The place was packed with tourists and I was forced to sit cross legged on the wooden floor right in the front row. The music began and a guy in this beautiful white dress with colorful skirts floated past. He absolutely reeked of alcohol, which is forbidden for devout Muslims. Sufi dancing is a holy dance where performers twirl in sustained circles. Dancers *whirl* in order to achieve states of religious ecstasy. The show began and this drunken man, a supposed holy man, in his colorful skirts began to whirl.

About five minutes into the whirling the drunken dancer starts to turn green. I see him heave subtly, like he's getting sick and then... he swallows it.

I can't believe it. I'm disgusted but also... captivated. Is this guy going to get sick? While he's performing? And then he does. He begins vomiting, but he doesn't stop whirling. He just keeps going. Whirling and vomiting, whirling and vomiting. And as he goes, he smears the chunks of vomit down onto his beautiful white dress so (thankfully) it doesn't fly out onto the audience. At this point from where I'm seated in the front row, my knees are pressed up against my chest, my face twisted in shock. I am horrified, but I can't look away.

Finally, he finishes his dance; but here comes the real takeaway, the part I want you to really absorb. After this drunken, barfing man who isn't exactly embodying the role of holy man, finishes a display that would humiliate most anybody else, he had the audacity to stand at the door and ask everyone for "Baksheesh" (tip in Arabic) as we all leave. He looked

CHAPTER IV - BOLDNESS

me dead in the eye as I passed him, his sweating face stinking of booze and an unpleasant chunk of something stuck to his lip, held his hand out, and prompted me, "Baksheesh?" His mood was confident and unapologetic, joyful even. His tummy probably felt much better.

I remember this nauseating story every time I'm afraid to ask for something. If there's a guy in the world who can show up to his job blackout drunk, vomit all over his nice clothes with an audience watching, and still expect to be rewarded, then, *queen*, I think you can ask for anything.

CHAPTER V

Persistence: Popping the Room or Eating It

In stand-up there are two extremes that we comics often talk about: *popping the room* or *eating it*. When a crowd has been rough all night and then one comic goes up and finally gets the room to really wholeheartedly laugh, we call that "popping the room." It's a little different than having a really great set because sometimes the audience is great for everybody, so it doesn't mean as much if you do well. There is something particularly satisfying when you get to be that one person who changes the temperature of the room. The one who finally manages to captivate an audience and gets them to really open up their mouths wide and laugh!

And then there's *eating it*, which is the dead opposite of popping the room. You don't get many laughs. You drip flop sweat and the room feels colder after you leave the stage. Probably, if they're smart, the host will go up after you and tell a few jokes just to reset the room. *Damn, I ate a bag of dicks,* you might say. Your face feels hot as if you'd just face planted into the pavement.

The challenging thing about stand-up comedy is that both popping a room or eating it are blatantly obvious to both the audience and the other comics. When I produce a show, running around and unable to listen to the comedian onstage, I can still tell without even trying how it is going. *Are they doing well or am I going to need to fix the energy before the next comic?* You don't even need to speak the same language as the comedian on stage. You will still know from the tone of the room whether it's going well for them or not.

And the wild thing is that it doesn't matter how many years you have under your belt. You can pop or eat the room on any given night. I think of the famous comedian, Jo Koy, when he infamously hosted the Golden Globes and it went less than stellar. This is someone whose career is so successful that they perform in stadiums. That is a rock star level comedian and even they can have an off night.

If you think about it, signing on for a career in comedy is signing up to potentially fail on bigger and bigger stages. So, what makes it worth it? How am I able to persist knowing that I might eat pavement? Because stand-up comedy has taught me not only how to take command of a room, but also when I fail, how to fail well.

It's How You Bomb that Counts

One night my comic friend Melissa and I drove an hour to Sebastopol for the Hopmonk open mic. My friend Jon Lehre runs it and I've always wanted to give it a try. When I saw the nicely lit stage and a few dozen people in the crowd, I was tempted to throw my new set out the window and retreat to my old jokes. *Oh, it would be so much more fun to kill with material that I know works!* But I didn't let myself do it. Nope! I was at an open mic for the purpose of pushing myself and trying new material.

My plan was that I would start with my opening joke that usually works and then I had three new premises to try. Sometimes my very best work comes out of throwing myself up there with my back against the wall. Words need to come out of my mouth. Something is going to happen. Sitting in the discomfort, staying true to myself, and seeing where I can take the set are all part of the exercise.

Well, it was uncomfortable. The opening joke went over alright but then my premises didn't get laughs or even chuckles. I kept going, paying attention to the audience, being present, doing a call back to something I'd heard earlier. Being bold. Taking up space. Taking up time. Until finally I got the light and launched into a closer I've been working on. It was a little more developed, so it got more laughs. I ended well and got off the stage.

Did I wish I had done better? Yes! My friend Melissa had a similar experience. And as we reflected on this in the car on our way back to the Bay I told her honestly, "Yeah I watched you kind of bomb."

"Ooof, I know; cringe, right?" she said.

"No, you weren't cringey at all, actually," I replied. "I was impressed. I think it's interesting to watch someone not get laughs because we all have sets where we bomb. You can really tell someone's level is how they handle those moments. I was paying attention to *how* you were bombing because that's so much more important in the long run. And you know what? You handled it like a boss."

She was steady and paused for laughs, even though they didn't come. She didn't make any excuses or abandon herself. She just went on to the next bit. She didn't rush either. She maintained a pace that was steady and confident. She stayed present to the room and what was going on around her. As she and I talked about it all afterwards, we ultimately decided we had done a fine job of not beating up on ourselves. We embraced bombing as a good workout. We had developed the self-acceptance muscle, which needs to be strong if you're going to keep going on stage, to keep going in comedy, and in life.

One of my favorite things is to watch a supposedly "really good" comic bomb and eat pavement. Because for me it isn't the fact that they don't get laughs that makes them truly bomb, it's *how* they bomb. I want to see how they handle it when things aren't going well. Are they going to start to retreat into themselves? Start to sweat? Do they rush onto the next thing? Do they stand their ground and enjoy themselves even when others don't find it funny?

You know the idea that you see a person for real when they are at their worst? That's what stand-up comedy does to you. It prepares you for the worst again and again and again.

In the beginning you bomb a lot and gradually improve. Your jokes get better and you get better at pivoting. With a lot of work, you have gotten better at failure.

When it comes to popping a room rather than eating it, I sometimes wonder if those wonderful successes happen on the precipice of failure. Have you ever sat outside during a tornado warning and watched the sky go green, watched the trees bend over sideways, and felt the eerie calm of something even bigger heading your way? The moments before the disaster are full of electricity. I think popping the room uses some of that electricity. A comic sticks their neck out a little too far, takes a risk outside their comfort zone, and the audience holds their breath for a moment in the tension, waiting to see which direction it will go. This charge, this electricity, manifests from a comedian's ability to wield what I like to refer to as the *Tempestas*.

In ancient Roman religion there is a goddess of storms or sudden weather called Tempestas. I love this idea of a goddess storming in and changing everything in a flash. It's a badass vibe. I think of her when I or another comic manage to warm up a room. It feels as though we're making weather happen.

CHAPTER V - PERSISTENCE

Inviting the Tempestas

The room was packed, sold out, but for some reason the energy was dead. I thought it might have to do with the fact that there was no DJ or overhead music at this venue. When the audience started to filter in it was quiet, so they felt like they had to be quiet, too. As a result, everyone huddled together at their tables in hushed conversation. After the show started, if the audience laughed at all, they laughed quietly. Each comic came onstage to swim upstream. I watched as every funny person (on any other night in front of other crowds) had made me cackle like an ornery fairy, but because of the weird atmosphere, their jokes didn't land. They were playing in cold empty space, with no ability to get traction.

Eventually it was my turn. Now I had done both great and meh sets at this venue, so it was anybody's guess how it was going to go. What I knew was that rather than terror, I had a lot of energy that night. I was there to have fun and I didn't plan on letting the audience's response deny me that fun! It was the perfect storm in a way: high energy (for me) and low expectations (from them). I tried not to pay too much attention or put too much weight on how the audience was responding. I decided that I would have fun no matter what.

When the host called me up, I walked towards the stage, but turned my upper body to face the audience. I smiled at them as though seeing an old friend I hadn't seen in a while and waved. As I climbed on stage and took the mic, I was careful not to oversell it. These mild-mannered folks were not going to be able to go from church vibes to rowdy mayhem on a dime. Better to connect with them first. Pull them in.

I said a loud and friendly, "What's up, Santa Rosa?" but also with just a hint of indifference and then I paused. I took in the room. I looked at faces. I watched them watch me. It took a second or two but it let them know I was actually observing them. People in the audience might have been thinking, "Oh, they can see me. I guess I'm a part of this, too. What if they say something to me? I'd better pay attention because, apparently, I'm involved." A few seconds. That's all it took. I made a few off the cuff jokes about the town. I was relaxed. I razzed them just a little bit. They loved it. They were ready to laugh. They just hadn't felt safe yet. I brought them in slowly and then we were off! My regular jokes went better than ever and I reduced some people to tears. All the comics afterwards congratulated me for "getting them." It doesn't always go this way for me, but when it does, I'm reminded that it's not only because the jokes are funny, but because I've learned how to change the temperature of the room. I've learned how to become the *Tempestas*.

The Difference Between Craft and Delivery

There is a craft to joke writing. Formulas. Setups and punchlines. Different devices you can employ to make your words as funny as possible. But there is also a craft to joke *telling*. And not just figuring out how best to tell the joke one time, but being able to connect with a room and customize the joke for each audience every time.

Very simply, you could call it reading the room, but I prefer the *Tempestas* because who doesn't like a goddess of storms?

The more I have performed and watched comedy the more I have started to see that there are two kinds of comics: The great joke writers and the great energetic powerhouses (i.e. *Tempestas*).

As with any performing arts like acting, dancing, music, there are artists who are more focused technicians and then there are artists who are more natural performers. The same is true of stand-up comedy; there are the types of comics who are skilled joke crafters and then there are comics who are skilled at reading the energy and playing to the room. The joke writers tend to focus on the craft of the words themselves, be more prolific writers and lean on the wit of the joke itself to get the laugh, whereas the energy readers lean more on their pure charisma and

CHAPTER V - PERSISTENCE

confidence to sell whatever it is they're saying. They're great performers. Very often comics are strong in either one or the other. But when you see comics who are doing multiple Netflix specials and becoming household names, you'll notice that they're good at doing both.

There are pitfalls to relying too heavily on either skill. An energy reader can change the temperature of the room when they walk on stage when they're in the mood to do it. But what if the energy reader is low on energy? Sad that day? Not able to muster it? Their jokes can fall apart like a house of cards without the right energy and delivery. That's why you need both.

Same with a talented joke writer. I've watched many clever joke writers bomb when the room isn't responding. They weren't connected enough with the audience or fluid enough to pivot or change up their energy. The craft of the words themselves can carry them far, but faced with a bustling or slightly rowdy crowd, they're unable to be dynamic; they're unable to cope.

My friend, screenwriter and director, Jade Raybin, calls these two things, "delivery and craft," but I would argue that changing energy sometimes requires more than just delivery. It's crafting on the spot. Sometimes, it's joke writing in the moment. It's flexibility. It's presence. And craft is more than just being clever; it's the meat behind the technique. The artistic integrity. It's not just the *how*, it is also the *what* that is being delivered.

Energy and Substance

Just as there are two levers at play to make great comedy, there are also two levers at play to make you a powerful queen. There's the energy you're giving and the substance of what you're saying—and when these two things are working together in harmony, they create a very powerful transmission.

115

Earthquake Woman is just one aspect of the *Tempestas*. It can be calm one minute and the next, *Tempestas* flocks in, dumps buckets of rain on everyone, and floods the streets. Likewise, she can bring sunshine, blow a breeze, and push the clouds away to create the most beautiful day in moments. She's dexterous like that. And so are you.

Being able to walk into any room and change the atmosphere is a power that was unintentionally given to women through the patriarchal structures that objectify and dehumanize us. Because of these structures we are forced into the role of performer and attention seeker in order to battle for our own safety or to pound on the glass ceiling—like a child of an abusive parent who has to learn how to read the room and change it as protection or an ambitious woman who knows how to play femme fatale. We elicit attention. And with that attention comes a certain kind of power.

As we step into our queen years, this attention becomes less objectifying or idolizing. The attention isn't necessarily coming from our body, our fanfare, our smile. It's coming from our ability to **connect**, our wisdom, and our ability to change the conversation. Our power gets an upgrade. We gather it from the way we align these two things: energy and substance or the integrity of what we are saying with the integrity of our energy behind it.

Have you ever talked to someone and their words were sweet, but it seemed disjointed from how they felt about you?

"Oh, Holly! You are looking so great today," their mouth says, but their face says that you may as well have rolled out of bed with toothpaste on your face.

There is a disconnect and you feel it. We've all seen it. They smile with their mouth and not with their eyes.

Humans are pretty sentient intelligent creatures. We can sense when a feeling isn't connected with the words coming out of someone's mouth.

CHAPTER V - PERSISTENCE

We can feel insincerity or doubt or secret hatred. Likewise we can feel someone being totally genuine. We can feel authenticity. And it can be one of the most powerful things in the world. When these two sides—delivery and material, energy and message—come together harmoniously it can cause an atmospheric shift, it changes the temperature of a room.

Why? Because it impacts how other people feel. It results in this elusive little concept called charisma. We often think of charisma as something that is reflected outwards, but in reality, charisma is how you make other people feel. I'll bet you don't even realize that it is something you can cultivate, but guess what? It's easier than you think.

Using the Weight of Charisma

A charismatic person isn't someone who has all the answers or traits that we desire. They are someone who is *reflecting back* to us those traits that we desire. Someone who gives us just enough of themselves to appear of substance and just enough space to reflect back those things we wish to project onto them.

Famous actor, Jim Carrey said in a commencement speech at Maharishi International University in 2014, "I realized one night in LA that the purpose of my life had always been to free people from concern." So that's what he decided to do onscreen and in his work. "I played the guy who was free from concern, so that people who watched me would be free from concern."

What stand-up comedy has taught me about charisma is that it is less about me and more about how I make other people feel. First and foremost, when people watch comedy, they want to laugh; they want to be free from care and concern. I can give them that when *I* feel that. When I'm having fun, they're having fun. When I'm feeling bold, it emboldens some part of them as well. There are times I'll be on stage, telling a story or starting a premise, on a precipice of a joke and their attention on me is palpable. It feels almost like a physical warmth coming at me in waves, like the feeling of sunlight paired with a gentle breeze. My presence to the sensation of this feels like a service. Like it honors the specialness of it. My enjoyment of it and my relaxation in that moment cracks open just a little more space for enjoyment and relaxation in them as well. The relationship a performer can have with an audience is an intimate one, an ongoing wheel exchanging pleasure and sensation.

Have you ever felt the pleasure a lover is feeling? Just because they're enjoying themselves it's as though you are sensing it too? Emotions are transferable and spread easily. In order for there to be emotional transference, there must first be connection: a willful giving over of one's attention. An established trust. So how do you first establish a connection that will allow people to feel your charisma?

For a long time, I thought the key was big and flashy: eye-catching makeup, funky fashion, being loud, etc. But now I realize it is so much simpler than all of those things and oh-so-much harder in many ways. Because it is a matter of physics, a matter of weight.

You Are Weighty and It's a Goddamn Blessing

As a lifelong dancer, recently I started learning zouk, a Brazilian social dance that's extremely flowy and highly technical—two of my favorite things. One day in class, the task was to switch between partners to learn the new steps. Suddenly, the zouk instructor popped in the line to dance with me and see how I'm doing. She is a petite Asian woman and I towered over her, but she was still commanding, her posture straight and movements sure. We began and after a few moments she scrunched her brow together and cocked her head to one side in confusion. Gently she shook my arms, and told me to give my weight over. I confessed to her that I'm self-conscious of the fact that I'm taller or bigger than her and most of the other women in the class. As a result, I'd been trying to hold my own weight, to not be too much of a burden or too heavy on anyone else. Without really acknowledging that comment, she simply told me that it feels "strange" to dance with someone who isn't giving the weight of their hands. She felt less of a connection. She couldn't fully sense if I was there or not.

How can she move with someone whom she can barely feel moving? It's like dancing with a ghost. You imagine they are there, maybe even sense a presence, but you don't know where they are. And that creates an uneasy feeling, doesn't it? That's exactly why we don't like ghosts. They are animated, but not living. They are present and not present. They are simultaneously popping into our realm and back out again and the only indication might be a cold feeling on the back of your neck. It's unnerving to interact with something like that.

And the same goes for you! Are you holding the weightiness of your being, physical or emotional, away from other people in the hopes of lessening their burden? Are you tiptoeing around like a creepy ass ghost?

When did we become so disconnected, so ill at ease with ourselves? When did we pick up this unhealthy belief that we are somehow a burden to others if we are weighty or of any substance at all?!

Well, I mean, as women, it is kind of baked in from birth. And whether you have been sent negative messages about your actual weight or not, my guess is that, as a woman, you have been fed some disempowering ideas throughout your life. Maybe you've been told you're *too big,* or *too loud,* or *too much! Too emotional. Get a grip!* There are a myriad of ways we are taught to shrink, to hold our own weight, to keep silent, to not ask, to not want. All along the way we are given the message that we must somehow reduce ourselves until we barely have any impact at all.

And that's the magic trick of the patriarchy!

Have no impact!

As a stand-up comic, I am unlearning this concept. I have to in order to be successful. I've watched national touring headliners at comedy clubs and one of the biggest takeaways is that these more famous comics are about 30% louder than most local comedians and when they speak every word is meaningful. Not as much rambling or fluff. Their content is tight. They are loud not necessarily in a flashy obnoxious way, but just in such a way as they make sure you hear every word because they've trimmed everything down so that every word matters. They take up space because they believe that what they're saying matters. As a result, they don't shrink from their impact. They make you listen!

And so, I make people have to deal with me. I shut the noise off in my brain and focus on the bliss of moving through space, hearing my voice, seeing and hearing its impact. Because I know now this is the work I have to do. To risk among others. To rely on others. To be impactful to others. To be a part of something more than myself.

To be motherfucking weighty.

The first queen lesson on the art of charisma and connection is to unlearn the messages that tell you to be less. Recognize them as bullshit when we see them. Otherwise, we are just bodiless ghosts, easy to ignore unless we rattle the windows and moan. Connection requires weight It also requires surrender. If you want to connect, you have to give your weight. You have to let go. You have to be willing to be a thing of substance.

So, what keeps us from being weighty? What keeps us from our natural charisma? It's the constant contortions to avoid failure. We shrink from our failures. If we are going to move forward, if we are going to be weighty and have impact—we must have a different relationship with our failures.

CHAPTER V – PERSISTENCE

> *"Don't lose too much weight. Stupid girls are always trying to disappear as revenge. And you are not stupid."*
>
> —Frida Kahlo

The Mistake: Attaching Ourselves to Failure When It's All Just Fireflies and Farts

The mistake we make with failure is that we tie it to our self-worth. We fail at an activity, or a project, or we have what feels like a great idea and it doesn't work out. Then we conclude it must have something to do with us.

What about that fart you left three paces behind you? You think that fart has something to do with you, too? Are you tracking that into the ethers? No, you let it go and you move far away from it. You don't want any association with it. You know what? That's smart. Treat your failures like a fart. *Pardon me, but let's all just pretend it didn't happen. Cough, cough. Oh look, some beautiful roses.*

Perhaps the biggest mistake we make with any creative output is that we attach ourselves too heartily to the end result. We are so proud so very proud of our creation. *I did a thing!* When it's great we stomp around like we're hot shit but we don't consider the flip side of that, which is that we take it to heart when it turns out badly. All of it: our failures and our wins—it's all catching fireflies in the zeitgeist. Sometimes we're lucky and we make it happen and sometimes it slips through into the ethers. Either way, we do our best and we become better craftier firefly catchers. Good for you. But you know what. You're just looking for that blinking light, swooping your net in midair and hanging on for dear life.

When you fail, don't take it too personally. Don't tie it to your selfworth. Don't get greedy. Don't send yourself down with it when it goes south.

In movies, when the captain decides to go down with the ship instead of trying to save himself, I always thought *what a waste. What a weirdo.* Fuck honor. Scramble out of that shit like a rat on a floating piece of driftwood. Tell ol' Rosie (yes, *Titanic* reference) to scoot the fuck over and make room for you. Don't go down with your own ship. Let that terrible presentation or that one bad judgement go down on its own. Let it sink to the bottom of the ocean where at least the bottom feeders can make a meal of it. Let them. Don't tie yourself to it. You are more than one moment. You are more than one bad call. You are more than even a whole bunch of years of bad decisions. There's something worth saving here and that is YOU. Don't go down on a ship when it's clear you can just build another one tomorrow.

The best thing about stepping into our queen years is your urge to do less because you've seen where all that *doing* has gotten you. Lots of farts and lots of fireflies, but where are you in all of it?

What if you didn't attach your sense of accomplishment to the outcome, but to the process itself? What if you were able to find a way to delight or even feast on your own failures?

The Contortion

You've failed at a thing. Wow, you mean like a human?! Yes, don't be cute about it. It stings. The mediocrity or straight up face plant is palpable and you know you should congratulate yourself for just doing the thing, but you can't help but feel

CHAPTER V - PERSISTENCE

disappointed. You aimed high and the outcome didn't quite match your vision. You beat yourself up. Maybe you even blame others. Worse than that, you feel compelled to tell anyone who will listen exactly how you messed up in great detail. People are shaking your hand, congratulating you, but their praise doesn't make it past your pissy attitude. You can't let it in. When someone gives you a compliment you secretly accuse them of lying and when they ignore you or don't say anything you think, "See? I knew it wasn't great."

Gradually people don't want to talk to you because you are too exhausting to be around. No amount of truthful praise or help seems to lift you up. Honestly, you are exhausted by yourself. You become so afraid of failing that you play it safe and retreat from your own creativity, not trusting that you have anything meaningful to contribute. You might even hide your failings from others because you don't believe you are worthy of love unless you win, you succeed, and you get everything right. Maybe you even stop trying altogether. Your anxiety builds because your spirit doesn't have a safe home in your body. You are contorting to avoid the scary feeling of failure, but some part of you knows the only way out is through. Some part of you can never stop wanting to try.

Finding the Yum in Failure

When I first started comedy, anytime somebody was bombing on stage one of my more veteran friends would mime eating a bowl of something with a spoon. Anytime I mentioned that I did crappy or was disappointed with my performance, he'd mime that and say, "You gotta eat it with a spoon. Eat it like it's great." It took me a while to really understand what he meant by that. He meant that not only was I *eating it,* but also that I was supposed to find a way to enjoy eating it. To eat it and say *yum!* I needed to embrace it and find delight in it.

Stand-up comedy has taught me not just how to fail and fail a lot. It has also changed my relationship with failure. Like we need to come up with a whole new word for failure entirely. Instead of slinking away from it, comedy has taught me to be as interested in my failure as my success. Eat your failure with a spoon. No matter what happens you are going to be okay. And that is a big shift in the queen years as well, recognizing that whatever happens you are going to be okay. We've failed a lot in life and we are still here to tell the tale. Why not revel in it a bit. Find ways to laugh at it and reap wisdom from it?

It's funny how much we want to twist and contort ourselves when we are faced with failure. It brings up all of our darkest shit. It asks us to feel embarrassed and ashamed. Unworthy. How could we be so dumb?! We attach our self-worth to the outcome. But what I'm proposing is not just about learning to fail. It's about almost liking it.

A failure is such because we label it so. Because we view our lives as a performance, because we burden ourselves with thinking we have to earn something to be acceptable, to be loved. We hold ourselves to high standards of perfection that we can never attain.

Finding the yum in failure is acceptance but also more than acceptance. Bombing is inevitable.

I had to learn this: I will do badly sometimes. People will at times not laugh. They won't get it. They won't listen. They won't care. Or they'll actively hate me.

The real bomb is when you give up.

CHAPTER V - PERSISTENCE

Failure is only a waste when you agree with those who don't get it. When you stop trying, that's a real loss. The learning is in doing badly and still being deeply interested in understanding why.

Here's the thing: So much of success is ultimately about continuing. One foot in front of the other. Yes, there are outliers who just seem supremely talented and everything is easy for them. Watch out for those talented and extremely lucky individuals and avoid comparing yourself to them. For most of us, the goods are earned through trial and error again and again and again. So, I ask you, what is more helpful in motivating yourself to try again and again? Judgement, comparison, and beating yourself up when you fail? Or objectively looking at your process and giving yourself credit for trying new things?

Using Discernment Instead of Judgement

Not only will this approach help you keep going (which in turn will help you get better), it makes you improve faster. In tennis if you shoot a shot too short, instead of saying, "That was bad," you say, "I noticed when I moved my body this way, that was the result." That is the difference between judgement and discernment. In the first one, you are assigning value to what happened (this is good/this is bad) and in the second you are assessing what happened. So, you're not judging yourself, you're analyzing the lab results. You're doing research. You're experimenting.

When you start training your mind to be more discerning, not only do you free yourself from the emotional turmoil and badgering, you are also more likely to notice more because you aren't clouding the moment with your judgment and the emotions that come from that. You are taking the growth from the moment instead of robbing yourself of it by substituting it with judgment. It makes it a little easier because there aren't stakes to it. You are giving yourself room to simply play. Let's try this. Instead of being focused on the outcome you are focused on the process.

Here's a piece of advice I got from a stand-up comic who after eight years had their first appearance on *Conan Late Night*. "Even when you start getting booked on showcases and in clubs, keep going to open mics. Don't stop working on your craft. Don't stop getting up as much as possible. Keep going even when it's going well. Especially when it's going well."

How often do we feel like there's one goal and once we achieve it, we're good? There's a tendency to want to back off once we've reached a milestone. And while I'm not saying we should "grind," as the younger comics like to call it. I mean, c'mon, the queen years are all about working smarter, not harder. There is something to be said for continuing to experiment, expand, and evolve even when we're already doing well.

What stand-up comedy has shown me is that persistence is important whether I'm succeeding or failing.

> The Wise Woman says, *"Keep going when it's good. Especially when it's good. Not in a pressured way. Not in a taxing way. But with the pure delight of exploration. You are a creature made for reaching."*

On any given night, I might be the one bringing in the *Tempestas* and popping the room or I may be just eating it, bombing my face off, but either way I persist. Persistence is the courage to do something again and again even when you know how badly failure hurts. Persistence is having the courage to keep going when it's good, because you know it could be even better.

CHAPTER VI

Attention: Waging a War

I became so still he couldn't look away.
Our gazes locked like two outlaws waiting for
the other to draw out their wallet. And pay.

We start out in life playing the fool when it comes to attention: longing for it, flirting with it, playing hide and seek with it. Then gradually as we learn its ways, attention becomes a device of war. We use it to dominate, manipulate, control and survive.

Just like any tool of power, attention can be used lovingly or pryingly. As an embrace or an attack. Attention is so powerful that you can use it to command someone else to do what you want. When you turn your attention onto someone, linking up with their breath, their eyes, their animal body you are able to tune into something primal that can hold them in place like prey.

Even the withdrawal of attention can be a power play. Like the narcissist who love bombs you and then ignores you or your frenemy in high school who paid attention to you when you were the new girl but then dropped you like a hot potato once someone cooler came along. We can get hooked on attention and then it becomes an addiction that masterfully erodes our self-esteem. Attention is a commodity and any relationship to it can potentially be a trap: being the predator or the prey, the controller or the controlled.

This war game of attention exists everywhere. It's woven into the very framework of the world we live in.

Companies spend tons of money paying attention to *you* in order to find new ways to get *you* to pay attention to them. Your own attention, your data, purchases, likes, tastes, and desires are mined through tracking apps. They find out what you care about, what you worry about and then they sell you things to attempt to make money off of your attention. They promote the feeling of *everybody's got one, gotta-have-it* and feed your mimetic desires all with the agenda to fatten their capital worth. In a capitalist society attention grabbing is used to manipulate our emotions, guide us towards problems that can be solved by buying something. Today, with even more outlets to capture attention and more people vying for it, we are bombarded with more and more demanding messages.

So naturally, if we are living in a world that operates with this combative relationship to attention, you can imagine it would also leak into any industry or professional arena where people are feuding for their paycheck, for their very survival, especially in a world where attention isn't just part of getting ahead in the game, but it is the game. Like in the performing arts. Like stand-up comedy.

CHAPTER VI · ATTENTION: WAGING A WAR

The Battlefield of Comedy

If you think using the analogy of war to talk about stand-up comedy is hyperbole, think again. In my first year of doing stand-up comedy, I saw three different fist fights break out at comedy shows between comedians and audience members. In my fourth year of comedy, I had a woman try to attack me after a show. The producer had to step in front of her to fend her off while I ran up the stairs and hid in the kitchen.

It all started with a little bit of attention: a simple compliment.

"Hey, you were great tonight," he said, his voice smooth and low. He smelled of chopped wood and Jameson and was handsomely dressed in a suit and a colorful tie. That one narrow strip of fabric looked more expensive than any piece of clothing I'd ever owned. He smiled like he wanted to make me aware of his generous lips. I was aware. I was very aware.

I laughed and replied, "Thank you so much!" This tall, smooth gentleman had followed me after I came off stage and cornered me in the lobby on the other side of the entrance.

He took his phone out of his coat pocket and slid it into my hand. He asked suavely like he already knew the answer, "Can I follow you on Instagram?"

"Oh, sure," I said, thinking, *oh a fan*. I relaxed a little. I was able to put him in a category. People asked to follow me on social media all the time. I blushed a bit, happy that someone thought I was good. Flattery will get you everywhere. As I took his phone and started typing in my Insta handle, I heard a woman's voice from the other side of the curtain. "What are you doing, *Valentino*?!"

My new fanboy, well fan*man* really, Valentino ducked behind the curtain, leaving me in the entryway with his phone in my hands. I finished typing in my Instagram handle, tapped the follow button, and respectfully closed the app. I stood there waiting for a few moments, thinking, *Hmmmmm. What am I to do? The man hasn't come back and I have his phone.*

I could hear him talking in low tones just on the other side of the curtain. He sounded defensive. I thought about just leaving his phone on the table in the entryway. *It'd probably be fine, right? Oof. But what if somebody takes it?* I was torn. I wanted to go back to the dressing room and relax but I was stuck holding this dude's phone. Finally, I spotted the edge of his table peeking from behind the curtain. I shrugged... *Why not?* I reached my hand around the curtain, set the phone gently on the table, and hoped the people arguing on the other side of the curtain wouldn't notice.

I was just turning to go when a tall goddess of a woman came charging into the entryway from behind the curtain. "What the *hell* were you doing with my man's phone?!"

I was contrite. "Oh no! You've got it all wrong. He just asked to follow me on Instagram!"

"What?!" She was incensed now. "Why do you think it's okay to hook up with my man over Instagram? What are you trying to do?" She thrust her finger in my face, her extremely long nails clicking threateningly. An image of an insect with pincers flashed across my mind.

"Oh no, you misunderstand," I said, "I'm an artist. People ask to follow me all the time."

By this time, the show was over and people were filtering out of the theater. Though people are passing by us, gawking, she wasn't quitting. It seemed to only invigorate her further.

"You shouldn't have another woman's man's phone in your hands!" she exclaimed. "That's not right. That's not right! You shouldn't be touching his phone! Who do you think you are? You little *bitch!*"

CHAPTER VI · ATTENTION: WAGING A WAR

Needless to say, I was embarrassed, but I was also starting to get pissed off. I felt Earthquake Woman rumbling beneath the surface. *Let me at her! Let me at her*!

"Listen, lady!" I spat loudly, just as I saw the producer of the show out of the corner of my eye. I lowered my voice, but I can't stop myself from saying, "I didn't know he was your man, for one thing. And besides, you're a total goddess! What are you worried about? Whatever it is, it has nothing to do with me. This sounds like a problem between you and your Valentino. It's not my job to control your man!"

With this she lunged at me, just as the producer stepped in front of her. Her nails just inches from scratching my face, I turned around and ran up the stairs behind me, down the stairs at the opposite end, into the kitchen, and then all the way into the back of the kitchen, startling a couple of short-order cooks. I plonked myself down onto a crate and began to cry.

So... there I go hiding and seeking again. As much as I relish the attention I get from being on stage, it does also attract unwanted attention or even unwanted competition with other women.

In that particular instance, attention became a commodity. Valentino was giving me attention which then pissed off his date. In her mind, attention is finite, something that there isn't enough of to go around, and it was inappropriate or even a call to war for me to accept the attention of another woman's man. Of course I didn't know Valentino was someone's date, but that's beside the point. Now consider that perhaps Valentino stepping away from her was some kind of manipulative chess move in his toxic relationship. He might have felt like he wasn't getting enough attention from her, so he gave me some attention, knowing it would get her attention. Oi! I didn't want that kind of attention! The contortions we make in order to get what we want can get really tangled as we drag other people into the mess!

So, as a stand-up comedian, do I go to war every day? Maybe not quite so dramatically, but I've definitely been through my share of battles and not always with audience members.

In show business, where every performer is scrambling for their big break, for their time in the spotlight, you see a lot of wild manipulating behavior. One showcase in particular comes to mind when I was performing at the Sacramento Punchline.

Bogarting the Producer

It had been a great night of comedy at Sacramento's favorite comedy club tucked away in the corner of a strip mall. All kinds of big names and touring national comedians have come through this club at one point or another, but tonight it was all local comedians: an all-woman showcase.

As female comics there is something wonderfully fun and also mildly annoying about all female showcases. They often have names like, *Girls Night!* or *Girls Just Wanna Have Fun!* They're annoying because of the infantilizing girls' idioms and also for the fact that there are many comedy shows that have all male comedians on their lineup but they don't call it *Boy's Night*. I wish they would. Why don't we see more all male lineups with names like *Beef Party, Circle Jerk, Boys Just Wanna Have Fun*? Probably because the male producers who book these shows consider this to be the norm: all male lineups. Most of the time they remember at the last minute to book one woman on the show to "keep it diverse." We female comedians quietly complain to each other about these Girl's Night shows. *Why can't they just have more women on a show and call it a regular show?* But at the end of the day, we're grateful for the booking.

The silver lining of these shows is that we get to hang out with a bunch of other women comics all night, not something we get to do normally because we are often the only woman or one of few women on any lineup.

CHAPTER VI - ATTENTION: WAGING A WAR

The backstage at these shows is usually quite lively and this night was no exception.

I was one of eight women comics, most of whom already all knew each other and had worked together, so the green room was bursting with a party atmosphere—all of us getting ready, catching up, touching up our makeup, and talking shit. We were cramped in the small but comfy backstage area scrambling over each other, our hot curling irons, and bags while drinking the complimentary cans of Liquid Death and energy drinks. The raucous energy among us also seemed to pour out of the dressing room and into the show. The crowd was ready to laugh and the comics one by one went on stage and all came off later glowing with satisfaction.

After the show, I was slow to leave the theatre—at any given show where I feel like I do well, there is the luxurious dance of farewell at the end of the night. I'm high on the laughter and high on the love and I don't want it to end. I love connecting with any audience members who want to chat with me and giving any last fist bumps or hugs with the other artists. So, I was doing my farewell dance, not wanting the night to end, easefully making my way towards the exit. One of the other comedians, Aria, was kind of keeping pace with me as I did this—also giving her share of goodbyes. Once I was nearly at the end of the hallway, I noticed the producer up ahead by the door at the same time as Aria noticed him. We both sauntered over, doing the kind of walk where we are each trying to keep pace with the other while trying not to look like we're trying. It felt more familial than competitive, almost like she and I were besties and we were going to say goodbye to him together. We sidled up to him and Aria started talking before I could open my mouth.

At first, I felt like I was part of the conversation because we walked up at the same time. I was listening to what Aria said. She thanked him for having her on the show and then proceeded to ask him a bunch of questions about his other shows. I was just standing there waiting for my turn. *Damn, I'd really like to thank him and get a sense of what else he can book me on too,* I'm thinking. So, I waited. And I waited. Politely, but she kept going on and on and on. She wasn't conceding her turn. It had been a couple of minutes of her talking. I looked back and forth from the producer's face to Aria, trying to stay in the conversation. When they laughed, I laughed and I even tried to dovetail into it. Conversations are like jumping rope; you gotta watch for the perfect moment to hope in and start talking without tripping.

"You know I feel the same way..." I began, but then Aria did something I will never forget. Without taking her eyes off the producer, she turned her back to me ever so slightly with a little sway of her body. Even though I was talking she didn't look at me. She kept her attention on the producer and pretended like I didn't exist. She refused to include me in this game of jump rope.

I trailed off.

Huh okay, I guess she's not done, I thought to myself. I was a bit annoyed so I glared at her—no one noticed—and I shifted my heavy bag from one side of my body to the other. I'd been lugging this bag around all day from work to this show. It had my change of clothes, makeup, extra shoes, and a heavy tripod in there. It had been a long day and I was tired and this woman wasn't yielding. In fact, she seemed to be intentionally ignoring me. I leaned from one side to the other. I sighed. I kind of bounced a little bit on my toes. It felt like she was really bucking social conventions by not giving me a chance to at least say a quick goodbye, but her energy was like a towering wall and I got the feeling that I could have been breakdancing and she wouldn't have even looked at me. It felt very calculated.

Now I noticed that over the course of the conversation, Aria had been inching her way closer to the producer, edging me out. I felt like I lost some kind of weird game I didn't know I was playing. At this point, I'd have better luck going to talk to someone else and swooping back in on him later, but I couldn't be bothered. I was tired and turned to go home.

That had been an interesting learning experience. I was simultaneously annoyed with Aria, *how freaking rude,* and also impressed. She used her attention to completely dominate this producer's attention and not allow anyone else in.

Encountering the Mean Girls

It is hard for me to imagine doing what Aria did. As much as I think of myself as bold and going after what I want, I don't care to do it at the expense of someone else: shutting another artist out as if that is going to make your own talent more noticeable. This was a contortionist costume I had tried on in the very early days of acting and I quickly realized it didn't suit me.

As I mentioned before, when I was 14 years old, I would go to Chicago to audition for acting jobs in movies and television. The way these auditions often work is you will be called in for a role based on your type. It doesn't matter how confident you feel about yourself, there is nothing more unnerving than walking into a room filled with talented people who are exactly your type. You look around and it's like staring into some kind of fun house mirror. It's you, duplicated many times over. You do a quick scan to see which one is the best version of you—and you never feel like it's *you*!

For me at that time my "type" was an attractive young girl next door. And sometimes the casting gets very specific. Often, I would open the door to the casting office and see a sea of about ten-to-twenty pretty brunette, blue-eyed teenage girls… all of them were at least 10 pounds skinnier than me. This was the waify '90s before JLo and Beyonce really made a case for curvy bodies like mine. All these skinny look-alikes lining the waiting room would look up from their scripts to size me up with their piercing blue eyes.

I'd glance nervously around as I'd make my way toward the sign-in sheet at the front desk. Any effort to look presentable felt like it melted away in the presence of these city girls with their fashionable clothes and chic haircuts. I'd sign in and self-consciously sink into a chair, silently motioning at my dad to sit somewhere else. Audition after audition I began to notice that there were three different ways girls seemed to handle this nerve-racking waiting room situation: there were some girls who seemed unconcerned with anyone else, barely glanced at anyone and studiously focused on their sides (pages from the script used for auditioning); there were a few girls who were mildly friendly, exchanging tight lipped smiles with me without moving their heads and then glancing back at their laps; and then there were the girls who were straight-up mean. These antagonists would take time and effort to look me up and down then scowl, laugh, or make a face of disgust. It was the worst. Their fierce looks would rattle my nerves and I would find myself stumbling over my words in auditions and forgetting lines that I knew I had memorized.

I struggled to know which one of these girls to be. In hindsight I was a timid friendly one; but audition after audition I'd get my nervous system stirred up by the mean girls. They'd rile me up into a sweaty self-conscious mess and then stride into the audition room confidently once their name was called. I wanted that confidence. I was tired of being chum for their pre-audition feeding time. So, one time I decided to try it. *Fuck it,* I thought. Maybe this was how it had to be in order for me to rise to the top.

I started studying the mean girls in movies like *Heathers*. This was before the movie, *Mean Girls*, came out but it didn't matter. That movie was a hit because it exemplified what was already happening in mainstream culture. We already had our plethora of mean-girl icons and I began

CHAPTER VI · ATTENTION: WAGING A WAR

doing a character study of them like they were my next role. The way they carried themselves, the cutting looks they executed, their dry delivery of put downs—I began playing around with these mean girl machinations.

The day of the next audition came and I steeled myself just outside the casting office. This time, not only was I not going to let myself get rattled by the mean girls but I was going to actively exude the attitude. I psyched myself up. *I am the best actress for the role. I am the It Girl and everyone else sucks ass in the wake of my pity for them!* I was going to nail this audition and more importantly, I was going to nail the waiting room!

I braced myself, chin up and stepped into the casting office. This time instead of self-consciously hoping no one noticed me, I scanned the room actively taking everyone in. One of the mean girls looked up at me with a tired look on her face like, *this bitch again?* I caught her eyes and held her gaze, *yep, bitch me again and you'd better watch your step*. She rolled her eyes and was the first to look away. *Victory!* I felt a fleeting sense of satisfaction countered by a slightly sick feeling in my stomach.

I signed in and took a seat. I probably should have looked at my script, but I was enjoying my new little game, so I scanned the room for more. I felt like I had a brand-new Jaguar and I wanted to take it for a drive. One of the studious girls noticed me staring and looked up at me. *Here it is! Here's my chance*, I thought. I slowly looked her over beginning with her shoes. (Have you noticed the mean girls always start at your feet? What is this? Some kind of predatory animal pattern?) I stared at her feet, moved my eyes up to her face, and raised my eyebrow at her subtly like, *huh, you look weird*. The studious girl looked down quickly and furrowed her brow. She gulped and started jiggling one leg. She looked... defeated. Shaken. Hurt. I did not feel victorious. I felt like shit. There was a heavy tugging in my chest. The nauseated feeling in my stomach grew. I felt simultaneously cold and sweaty, like I was burning up inside, but my skin felt chilled like I was just dipped in a cold plunge. And then... my name was called.

I tried to breathe. I gathered my script—I hadn't even had time to review my lines—and walked into the casting room. To say I had a bad audition that day is to put it nicely. Already flustered and sweaty from my experience, I struggled to ground myself and connect with the character on the page. I had worked so hard to get myself into mean-girl mode that I had a hard time shaking that rancid attitude and accidentally snarled a bit when I was stating my name.

When I fumbled over a line, instead of continuing on like I was trained to do, I rolled my eyes at myself and sighed in exasperation. After the first run through the casting director, who knew me pretty well by now and was used to my typically sweet mild nature, was confused by my newfound attitude, but still hopeful. She asked me to do it again but this time looking less at the sides. I tried a second time and it was worse. I forgot lines, took long awkward pauses, and flipped my hair around nervously. There was nothing cool or confident about it. I had one of the worst auditions of my young career.

After that, I learned my lesson. Being a mean girl was not for me. It required too much energy and absolutely ruined any innate talent I might have had to bring to the craft. I eventually found my own mode of being in the audition room. I became openly friendly. *Fuck worrying about who was going to get the part!*

I was surrounded by other young actors all going through the same fight to get into this business. There was too much to learn from each other! From that moment on I would openly look around at who was there, but with a friendly smile. I'd come super prepared, having spent time fleshing out my character and memorizing my lines and I leaned on that for my confidence.

If the mean girls looked at me sideways, I just ignored them and felt a little sorry for the effort they were taking to hate on me. Instead, I'd introduce myself to the timid, friendly girls and found we could

CHAPTER VI · ATTENTION: WAGING A WAR

chat easily: asking each other who did our headshots, swap tips about different casting directors, *Oh Wyatt and Brown hates it when you don't have every line memorized,* and talk about the trials and tribulations of being a young actor. Some girls had been in it since they were babies before they ever really had a choice, others were more like me and had to beg their parents to let them get into it. Every story was different, but we all faced the same plight: never-ending auditions, studying on trains, buses and late at night to stay on top of schoolwork, constant rejections, constant pressure to stay thin and pretty. Not only did I find a new approach to the audition room through this experience, but I learned early the benefit of finding sisters in show business.

So, you're not going to catch me trying to be a mean girl, push other artists aside, or bogarting a producer's attention in a social setting. I came across it again and again when I was an actor, then again as a professional dancer, and now I see other comedians do it to each other all the time. I just roll my eyes. I learned when I was 14 years old that nothing good comes from waging a war against other artists as if they might steal something from you. My own attention is a precious currency that deserves to be focused on my own craft, not on dominating other comedians. *Your peers are not your audience!* All that being said, there are spaces where I don't hesitate to dominate....

Using Attention to Dominate

Now this is the part of the book where you and I are in the trenches together. We recognize the war going on and we're hanging out in the fox hole telling stories about our near-misses and our sick-ass scars. I'm about to tell you some of my war secrets and I'm a little worried you'll judge me for facing you while holding the weapon behind my back all this time. For as much as I want to be holy and pure in my intentions (Wise Woman, hello!), there's the blatant fact that I've been controlling audiences all along. It is my job. A performer's role is to entrance and inspire. We're like hypnotists or magicians. We make your worries disappear for a few hours and take you into another world. Learning how to capture your attention is a part of that. On good days, it is not violent, nor a battle of any kind. However, things like dominance and manipulation have their purpose.

It starts before I even say a word.

When I step on stage, there is one thing I always try to remember to do. It is the most important thing. If I can remember to do it, it changes how the whole rest of the set goes for me entirely. The moment I begin to walk on stage I begin to look into the sea of faces and start noticing details. I am starting to connect with them immediately. There is often a split second of slight disconnection as I navigate steps or the edge of the stage, as I finagle the microphone off of the stand and make sure the cord isn't caught. But the moment I am able to, and right before I speak, I am putting my attention on the audience. I am establishing a connection. I am establishing dominance through my attention.

Kasia Urbaniak, a former dominatrix turned empowerment coach talks about this in her book, *Unbound: A Woman's Guide to Power*.

> From the dominant state of attention, you can locate the other person-figure out what's going on with them-and help them to locate themselves. You can ask for anything. And because attention out gives you exquisite sensitivity to the reactions of the other person, you can surf their resistance until you arrive at a solution. This is how you lead another person, heart, mind and soul.

I'm not just looking at the audience and thinking about myself. No. I am looking at them and putting my full attention on them. I see them. In my mind I try to scan the audience and point out facts. It has to be quick, so it might be thoughts like, "Holding a glass, round face, table

CHAPTER VI · ATTENTION: WAGING A WAR

of all ages—looks like family—over to the right." You'd think this would be easy to do, but when you're going on stage your nervous system can begin to bang and clang all of its bells, and you are naturally inclined to put your attention on yourself, not on others. But the problem with this is it makes you feel self-conscious. The point of this exercise (observing and thinking three facts) is to get my focus off of myself and establish a connection with the audience. If I'm lucky, something funny about them springs to mind in the moment and I'll get to say it before I can think too much, which seals the connection. It is a way of establishing trust: I am here. in this moment with you. I've got you. I am establishing the flow of attention.

I'm dominating you, but you know what? Y'all like it that way.

Once the audience feels me seeing them, they relax. Something about this sets them at ease and lets them know that they can allow me to lead them.

Harnessing attention as a queen is a craft that is invisible when done correctly. When I'm performing, I'm using my platform to guide people's attention, usually to things that make them happy and make them laugh, but occasionally I hit a nerve and it does the opposite. A person's attention shifts inward towards their feelings and their own shame or anger rises to the surface. Now a war has been launched that I didn't even intend to start. And I have to battle using attention as my weapon. I can pull my attention away and see if they peter out. I can try to direct their attention somewhere else. I can put my full attention on them, pepper them with questions, and dominate them. There are many ways to wield attention in war. Withdrawal, domination, manipulation. Attention can be used to heal or to fight. And sometimes you'll need both.

You've heard the phrase, "Pick your battles," and it couldn't be a better time than now in your queen years to begin assessing what wars you're waging. The fight to reclaim territory that is our own bodies? Pushing back the invaders of our own desires? Throwing up defenses to protect our precious time and attention? This begs the question: When I go to battle on stage, what do I stand for? What is the fight for—other than your attention? In some ways I'm an avatar for every woman, presenting an example of what it looks like to be free of concern like Jim Carrey, fighting the good fight out here against shrinking, against self-doubt and against shame.

Wow! Sounds great! Yes, I can do this! Why would I ever do anything else? Whatever could ever get in my way? Well, there is one thing that keeps us from being willing to fail, a little thing that's rampant in our world: Shame.

It's monolithic, yet also often hidden. It's tucked away deeply and yet somehow leaking out of us everywhere. It's a cheek-burning, breath-swiping, heart-stinging, Christmas-carol-singer-knocking-on-our-door-and-demanding-we-listen kind of cringe. And if we are to become the queens that actually make waves in this world, we have to learn how to step over it like a pile of dirty laundry that isn't ours.

We must learn to cultivate shamelessness.

CHAPTER VII

Shamelessness: Working the Crowd

I can't get drunk anymore, because every time
I wake up the next morning feeling so much shame,
like I did something bad, but I don't know what it was.
Like I must have just dipped my genitals in mustard
and smeared 'em on somebody's white couch.

If attention is a tool of war, then shame is psychological warfare.

You're too much!

Behave yourself!

Don't try to outshine the boys, they won't like you.

Over the years, I've gradually made myself less available to these kinds of messages by seeing them for exactly what they are: psychological

143

warfare. Covert in their tactics, they can slip right past the guards if you're not careful.

Have you ever had someone ask you, "Can you hold onto this for a second?" and you instinctively reach out for the thing they're trying to hand you? That's like shame. You reach out for it instinctively without recognizing what you're being handed. Without understanding its nefarious consequences. We're tricked into holding it like a game of hot potato. Everyone just keeps passing it around trying to fob it off on someone else for fear it will burn them and leave a mark.

In its sneaky way, shame works on us to instill ladylike propaganda, conditioning us from a very young age. As I'm stepping into my queen years, working to locate my own desires and things that stand in the way of them, I also find myself locating instances of shame in my childhood memories. They'll float to the surface of my consciousness like a dead body.

I was 12 years old and hanging out with my friends in my parent's living room: me, my best friend Leah, and these three boys we'd met at her church group.

The boys were athletic and on their school's gymnastics team. I was also super athletic, a dancer who took ballet, tap, jazz, and modern. So, at some point in the conversation we started comparing our athletic prowess and, in particular, doing the splits.

One of the boys was showing off. "Normally I've got past splits, but..." He slid easily into splits onto the floor. "I've got to warm up to go any further than this when I'm, y'know, cold."

Not one to be outshone, I didn't let the fact that I was wearing a skirt at that moment hold me back. I slid onto the floor as well, legs stretching apart while holding my skirt down tautly so it wouldn't creep up or flash my underpants. I thought I was being demure. Once I was fully in the splits I looked up and smiled at the boys with a smug look.

CHAPTER VII - SHAMELESSNESS

The older boy shot a look of disgust at me and reprimanded me with a kind of parental scolding to which I wasn't accustomed,

"Get off the floor," he hissed. "Act like a lady!"

The words hit me along with a wave of shame so sudden and fierce that I scrambled up from my position on the floor hurriedly re-adjusting my skirt the whole time in order to maintain decorum.

That incident has stuck with me all this time.

The feeling of that shame.

Do you ever wish you could go back and do something over? Do you ever feel like you don't know what to do in the moment, but then the moment you leave you think of the thing you wish you would have said?

I wish me and ol' Earthquake Woman could go back to that day and tell that boy to fuck off. Or I wish my Comedian could have done something wild like take my skirt off entirely, do the splits, and say, "Oh yes, that's so much easier without the skirt!" Or maybe this was an opportunity for Wise Woman to stare this young man in the eyes and school him on what was what. I wish. I wish. I wish.

Stand-up comedy is teaching me there's no need to wait for the wishing after. The Comedian is teaching me to go after the punchline to begin with, to be direct, and most importantly, to not be available for the hot shame potato. To not open my arms instinctively when it's lobbed my way.

Shame can act like a big pause button that hijacks our nervous system and makes it difficult to speak. Shame in the past has left me stunned and silent. Like I said, it's warfare. But stand-up comedy is teaching me to dodge that rain of bullets so I can say what I want to say in the moment. It's teaching me shamelessness.

It's not just a comedian that has to deal with this, it's every queen. Every single one of us. The world will easily control you by making you feel like you have to apologize, feel embarrassed, and take responsibility for other people's feelings. They will control you by making you feel like you have to be *nice*.[3]

De-conditioning the Nice Girl

Here's the slow torture of being conditioned to be nice: My stand-up comedy bits come to me most often when I'm half asleep. An entire bit will just flood my mind and I'll roll over and scramble for some paper and a pen to jot it down. This is an infuriating way to create. *Comedian, can you please talk to me when I'm awake?!* But alas, when I am awake my conditioned mind has taken control and those raw jokes can't make it past the Nice Girl filter. Sometimes when my writing is going more slowly than I would like, when I question whether I am funny or not, I have to remember the deep and deliberate conditioning I've received. The nice-girl conditioning my entire life that I've only recently begun to unravel myself from'. It's tricky to be "nice" and also leave your mind open for poking fun, blurting out the elephant in the room, or saying what you really think. My brain hasn't been wired for it.

As I mentioned earlier, the nice-girl conditioning has never lent itself to anything innovative or profound or hilarious, so I realized pretty quickly that my comedy writing had to find a way to duck around the Nice Girl conditioning. I am slowly rewiring my brain for it now when I do stand-up comedy. There is a funny, provocative girl in there who has been suppressed for decades. Is it any wonder I write best from my subconscious and from those moments when I am not thinking of being funny, but I am just letting the Nice Girl lift up her proverbial skirt?

---

[3] Nice is different than kind. Nice in this context is about making things pleasant for other people while sacrificing yourself. Fuck nice. But I still prioritize kindness and compassion.

CHAPTER VII - SHAMELESSNESS

What enrages me is how effective shame can be and how hard it can be to shake it off. But let us not forget that it is something that we can refuse to let in.

Shedding that shame becomes essential in the queen years. It's a mission we must take on in order to propagate the garden of our self-love. Many women I know experience an uprising of shame-related feelings as they approach their late thirties and early forties, if only because they've experienced life, they've learned lessons and now they may know better about some situations in their previous lives. As our hormones shift like the ground beneath us, we can be haunted by our prior worries, past regrets, embarrassment, and shame. As we see and recognize the patterns, we can dig in deeper until we have shame about the shame! We spiral. But I don't think these shame spirals get louder because they're meant to haunt us forever, but rather so we can heal them, release them and take our self-love to a stronger frequency. These charged shame spirals are a bit like cystic acne that lies deep under the skin. They are trying to work out the pus and the gunk and in order to bring all of that to surface and get it out.

The Contortion

You could write a whole novel based on the stories that run through your mind when you lie awake at 3am and can't get back to sleep. Your past holds you hostage. As a result, you are settling for less in your life than you should: when someone

> treats you badly you apologize to *them*. You somehow feel like it was probably your fault. When you aren't given the promotion or your work goes unacknowledged you burn with embarrassment. You are constantly consumed with what other people think of you. Or you become a perfectionist. Your nervous system is constantly scanning the horizon for threats to your plan. You believe if you can just get it right moving forward then somehow you will settle down and feel some sense of normalcy. You don't put yourself out there in any way because it feels like a threat to your very existence. At your core you feel deeply convinced that something is wrong or different about you that cannot be fixed. The thought makes you collapse, but what gets you back up again is anger. Some part of you knows you are living out a program that was installed since birth and it's frustrating; but in your fight with yourself, you do everything else but the one thing that will help: accept yourself.

I Just Want to Take a Shit

The answer to my shame coming to the surface was to get on stage and start talking about stuff.

> *"Oh ho! You feel bad about something! Embarrassed even? Let's share with a roomful of strangers!"* says the wicked self-torturing gremlin inside every comedian alive.
>
> This method is a bit like picking or pressing on a pimple. It doesn't always make it go away any faster, but it does get stuff moving.

CHAPTER VII - SHAMELESSNESS

Getting up onstage is where I realized how infectious shame is.

Stand-up comedy is a platform to speak to all kinds of embarrassing things: Comics have permission to point out those relatable things that no one usually talks about. We love identifying and naming the awkward commonalities among us that usually go unrecognized. Acknowledging these things out loud has always felt like a healing aspect of the art. In the words of the famous shame researcher, Brené Brown, "Shame needs you to believe that you're alone... Shame thrives on secrecy, silence, and judgment" (*Atlas of The Heart*). So, when we are able to say these things we normally hold in silence as shameful in front of a whole group of people and laugh at them together, the charge of them is released. People hopefully leave feeling a little lighter, a little more like they belong, and a bit more sense of worthiness.

But it's also not as straightforward simple-pimple as it sounds. For a long time, I said a lot of these embarrassing things on stage and *did not* get laughs. It did *not* free people of shameful feelings. In fact, it did quite the opposite. Sometimes the temperature in the room would forcefully turn against me—a chill would enter and I felt like the great Tempestas of the Long Winter. Or the shocking things I said would just have a middling effect. The audience might chuckle nervously, gasp, or groan in reaction, but it wasn't exactly the spit-take level of spontaneous laughter I was hoping for. It didn't feel *good*. I knew I was on the right track, but I couldn't figure out how to make this work. In my ambitious mind I was trying to execute the greatest sleight-of-hand magic trick of all time: Wise Woman was exorcising the people of their darkest pain and getting paid in free drink tickets and stage time! What a mitzvah! What a service I was providing! All the while thinly veiling it behind the Comedian's playful jokes.

"How come I wasn't able to free these freeloading free-comedy-show goers of their shame? Don't they know what was good for them?!"

Earthquake Woman roared.

Time after tedious time, I tried. I fiddled. I pondered. It took me a long time and a lot of tweaking to realize where I was going wrong... and it happened with this one punchline.

It's just a tag to a joke, a bonus joke that goes after the first punchline. This particular tag goes at the end of a story about spending the night with a man and waking up to him the next morning. I look at his face in bed next to me and realize this is my moment. To ask him for what I want. I'm nervous, but I have to be brave and vulnerable so I tell him earnestly, "Ummm. what I really want is for you to goooooooo!" I wave my hand in front of him like I'm trying to execute a magic trick to make him disappear.

The audience laughs at this twist. And then I add the tag, "Because what I really wanted was to put on my reading glasses, look at my phone, and take a shit!"

Another surprise. Bit of shocking honesty. And the audience got it, sort of. I mean so many of us can relate to the desire for everyone to just *go away* first thing in the morning so we can do our business in peace? It's a basic human experience, but it really didn't get the full buy-in laughter that I was looking for. I wondered, *Was it too gross? Was that what wasn't working?* But, damn it, I knew I had heard other comedians do jokes that were grosser than this! And they were successful—so I decided it might be in the delivery.

I began to play with how I was saying it. At first, I would kind of wince when I said "shit," thinking I should communicate that I also thought that this was gross. But not only didn't it work, it made it worse. Looking out at the faces in the audience, they would sometimes even mirror my wince as I said it. It would kick off a kind of shame wave that would spread around the audience like wildfire.

CHAPTER VII - SHAMELESSNESS

The feeling of shame from me infected the crowd and tampered with everything else I said on stage after that. It was a hard feeling to shake once I ignited it. It was like dropping poison in the water. But how else should I say it? To me, it felt nicer (Aha! There's that word again!) to let them know I was a lady who didn't want to have to take a shit, but that little wince and admission in my energy didn't actually help them hear it at all! Instead, it transferred that shamefulness to the entire crowd.

It wasn't until this one time when I literally almost forgot to say it... I got to the end of the bit forgot that there was more until I felt the tension, and then in that moment I remembered the line and just said it in a matter-of-fact way, almost throwing away the line completely with no emphasis, no facial expression, no emotion, most importantly *no shame*, just as if I was saying it to my sister standing right next to me.

"*I really just wanted to put on my reading glasses, look at my phone, and take a shit.*"

And with that delivery, the audience *exploded*: a man pounded his hands on the table in back and I watched as the bodies in the front row waved forwards and backwards like a synchronized prayer of mirth. The wave came toward me and splashed across my heart. I felt elated, like I had just unlocked a whole new level to the game.

And that's when it clicked. The admission of shame had been killing it all along. The trick to saying whatever you wanted on stage was to do it *shamelessly*. To own it with your whole being.

Shamelessness is necessary for working a crowd because an audience will want to reflect any and all of their feelings and hang ups that come up for them while you're talking up there. They will want to project their embarrassment and shame all over you. And I just keep my hands to my sides when that happens. I'm not available for that.

This joke, and other jokes like this, are how I have come to realize that my job as a comedian isn't just to talk about things that people don't normally talk about. It is to release people from their shame. And I can only do that when I model that shamelessness myself.

Shame may be infectious, but the opposite is also true. A kind of shamelessness can pop the pimple of other people's shame. In order to dodge the bullets of the psychological warfare that is shame, we have to learn how to de-condition that Nice Girl. We have to put so much power in her hands that they are no longer available for the hot shame potato that people want to hand her. But how? Where? In what way do we actually practice this?

Apart from getting on stage and telling your dark secrets to a roomful of strangers—I don't recommend it for most people—how does a queen practice shamelessness? How does a queen learn to become less available to other people's projections? How does a queen learn to share themselves without the charged emotion that we're doing something innately wrong or not nice? How does a queen just learn to be, to feel, to stand in their worthiness? I think the secret is in sisterhood.

A Queen Sheds Light on Shame

If we are to truly step through the burning ring of fire of mid-life and walk out the other side a transformed queen then we have to begin to let these old pieces of ourselves, including shame, be released. And the only way is to allow them to be seen. The answer is in sharing our experience with others trusted not to judge us. Our sisters. Our besties. Our girlfriends. Those people who can hold non-judgmental space for us are worth their weight in gold! We have to make time to talk to each other and share our stories, so we can understand our experience is often a shared one and let the shame morph into laughter.

Shame contorts us inward, focusing all of our attention on our own pain, our own striving and failings. Shame can suck you into such a contraction of self-involvement that you become completely oblivious to

CHAPTER VII - SHAMELESSNESS

the pain of others. Which is why it's enormously important to have allies and trusted friends whom you share with and whom you allow to share with you. When you are focusing on others with empathy it annihilates the shame in you. It cannot breathe without your attention to it.

> "Shame is a social emotion. Shame happens between people and it heals between people"
>
> —Brené Brown, *Atlas of the Heart*

Now here's the tricky part: We are often encouraged to *Just do it. Go for your dreams, put yourself out there, be bold! Dance like no one's watching! Don't be afraid of looking like a fool, just go for it!* But the deep fear that keeps us from doing that is the fear that we will be mocked, embarrassed, and all of our best tries and hard work will be summed up as mediocre at best, a huge embarrassment, or—worst of all—offensive. Just the threat of feeling shame can make it impossible to try or force us to shrug off the attention when we do.

If speaking our shame is the answer to freeing ourselves of its imprisonment, then what keeps us from speaking up? Judgment, mainly. We fear revealing something only to be left out in the cold, open air, with no allies.

> "We all carry around the flotsam and jetsam of perceived humiliations that actually mean nothing. We are a mass of vulnerabilities, and who knows what will trigger them?"
>
> —Jon Ronson, *So You've Been Publicly Shamed*

As a queen you are naturally experiencing new things: your body is changing, your brain, your life experiences. These things are inevitable, but what's important isn't that we are experiencing them, it is how we choose to frame them and live in them. Are we going to allow ourselves to feel like we need to hide in shame during the process? Or is there a way to embrace them and live shamelessly through them?

Words remind me of birds. They are small and compact when they stand still inside of us, but when we say them out loud, they unfurl and take flight. And to me that's what's so very powerful about sharing our stories in the company of trusted allies. These stories are sometimes a window into our very private inner-most thoughts, secretive shameful thoughts that once let out of our mouths fly about the room and change form. Shame thrives in the darkness. Our stories of embarrassment untold sit in our bowels and seethe with poison. But learning to laugh over them allows you to let them go, knocks the stink off, and lets the light in.

Not only are we helped when we share our stories, but we are helped when we hear others stories as well.

Throughout our lives as we reach for attention from others, we are reaching for our sense of belonging, our sense of self, of connection and in an effort to get those things we wear any number of costumes: the Nice Girl, the temptress, the bad girl, etc. Even motherhood as you are faced with watching your child go out in the world and be judged against other kids, comes with its own posturing and outfits because now not only is your own worthiness and belonging being fought for, but your child's as well!

All of these costumes start to strip away when we begin entering our queen years. (They're too hot and the shoes are uncomfortable anyway!) As our chemical armor comes down, we are too uncomfortable to give a shit, or put up with shit, or deal with anyone's shit! All the shit gets left in a pile with the costumes and, if we're lucky, that's where we can leave our shame as well, recognizing it was never a part of us, but a contortion that came with trying to fit into the damn outfit.

And I think that's key in this whole process of stepping over the shame piles: identifying those other queens who can hold space for it—*Nay!* That *love* you for it. Not everyone needs to extricate their shame on stage like me, but you need to find friends who are down with it. Maybe they've experienced the same type of shameful things, but not necessarily. They are friends who are simply able to have empathy for your experience.

When we are with people who are able to hear these stories of shame and not judge us, we are able to identify what is actually us and what was just a costume that we had tried on. Whenever I imagine taking off all of these costumes, I just imagine layer after layer coming off and the form underneath shrinking from all of the unraveling and finally revealing a sweet lumpy center with the consistency of warm marshmallow. Underneath all the layers of disguise we are loving, a bit formless, sweet and gooey. Through the compassionate eyes of our friends we get tuned in to the sweet lumpy center of ourselves. We are in touch with the oneness that we all come from.

The form we take may vary from one day to the next. One day we might feel like the sweet gooey love lump, and another we might feel like the fire spitting Earthquake woman, but either way the core of us, the center is the same. So how do we get in touch with the truest version of ourselves? How do we stand in our worthiness?

I've established that shame is contagious. There is nothing worse than feeling the creeping embarrassment from a performer who isn't managing to have fun on stage. The same can be said for all of us in everyday life. So, somebody has to take the leap. Someone has to go first in their shamelessness. We have to look for models of shamelessness. And when we can muster it, we must model it for others.

The Shameless Type Who Gives No Fucks

If shame is taking something on, like a hot potato, then being shameless is giving something back. Your hands aren't available because they're full of something you're about to throw. You're emanating a power like Wonder Woman and her bracelets. And that something that you're emanating is, at its core, a picture of worthiness.

You've seen this shameless person at the party. All eyes stare in disbelief as they act accordingly and instantly on what they want. Someone needs to be the one to start filling their plate. If they're hungry, they don't think twice about it. They need a ride home, they'll ask anyone who is going their way. This person isn't seen as distasteful to others because they are so confident in their actions, so clean and supple in their asking, clearly not caring too much what other people think, that we all admire them. And if someone else *does* deign to find them distasteful, they don't notice. What does it matter to them? This shameless person is so deeply okay with themselves that it's as though just being around it makes us feel okay, too. This don't-give-a-fuckery—so long as it is paired with a healthy dose of empathy and awareness of others around them—can be an enviable trait.

Shamelessness says, *Even if I mess up, it's okay because I am not what I do.* Shamelessness says, *My value has nothing to do with how successful or productive I am. My value is inherent. I am worthy without conditions.*

What follows from that belief is a confidence that sounds like, *I'm not afraid of falling and looking silly because hopefully if I do, you'll laugh along with me... and, hey, even if you don't I will, and I'll be okay with that.* The allure of shamelessness is that it doesn't just make you feel free, it gives others permission to feel shameless as well.

CHAPTER VII - SHAMELESSNESS

Writing Your Book of Possibilities

Over the years, I've shed more and more constraints and learned how to give fewer fucks but I couldn't have done so without knowing other bold, shameless women who paved the way.

I'm sure you can remember a time you witnessed someone doing something shamelessly and even if you thought to yourself, *tsk tsk,* you secretly were impressed by their bravado? When those things happen, they get filed away inside our minds into what I like to think of as a kind of catalog or *Book of Possibilities* that we add pages to whenever we witness new acts of bravery, boldness and shamelessness.

I have this philosophy that when I do things that are not considered "ladylike" onstage (Uhhh… most everything. Have you *seen* my act?) it doesn't necessarily have to be something that all women watching would agree with, cheer on, or think is inspiring; but I do want them to feel a little stretched by it. I want their perception of what they think a woman can and should do to be stretched even if only a little bit. Being in a position where we are experiencing things our culture doesn't want to talk about, we are in a particularly powerful position: We can either spread the shame disease or we can add to other people's *Book of Possibilities.*

When we witness other women doing things that we wouldn't dare to do, our worlds expand. What we think of as okay or permitted gets stretched out and we are left with a bigger world. Throughout my life I can think of those times when I watched a woman I know do something that blew my mind just a little bit or a lot. These don't have to be wild things. They can begin with small things from the women in your family:

My Aunt Patty was a legend in my family. The story goes that when she was a young girl, she and my mom would ride their horses to school in rural Illinois. Aunt Patty had the most stubborn horse and would cuss out that animal every day on the way to school. My mom testifies that she learned how to swear from listening to Aunt Patty cuss out a horse. My mom's story was corroborated by my experience. The Aunt Patty I knew would often say, "*I don't give a damn.*" and you could tell she meant it. This may not mean much by today's standards, but she grew up in a time when ladies didn't say things like this. So, my sister and I would widen our eyes and chuckle with glee when we heard these words spit out of Aunt Patty's mouth. She was feisty and bold and definitely expanded my *Book of Possibilities*.

Once my mom was visiting me from Indiana. It was myself and a few other performer friends and our families hanging out on a river in Nevada City in California. California has a hot tub culture, where if people want to swim and they don't have a bathing suit, they'll go in their birthday suit. It's pretty normalized here, but I was a bit worried about how my Mid-Western mom would react to seeing all of us strip off our clothes as we approached the river. It was hot so the clothes came off on all of us younger folks pretty quickly. No fussing about shyly. Straight to skinny dipping. I waded into the river and was in for a surprise when I turned to look back only to see my 73-year-old mom, whom I never imagined doing such a thing, stripping down to her panties. The rest of the afternoon my mom basked in the sun and frolicked freely in the water in her huge cotton underwear. I was simultaneously aghast and also secretly impressed. Having inherited her voluptuous body type, seeing her embrace her aging curves helped me embrace mine.

Perhaps one of the earliest and most powerful things I witnessed was when I was a teenager and I went to see Tori Amos for the first time.

When I was 16 years old, I went to see the singer-songwriter in concert. It was my very first music concert and I went with my older sister, Heather, and my best friend Shannon. I have a very distinct memory from that concert, watching this beautiful goddess of a woman writhe sensually on a piano bench. She straddled that thing, threw her head back as though she were having a full-body orgasm. It was so sexual and sensual and

CHAPTER VII · SHAMELESSNESS

shameless! She was tiny, but she made herself seem huge. It was clear to me that she was at one with the music and the song, that there was an energy coursing through her that I somehow recognized.

I asked my sister, "How old is she?"

She answered, "I don't know, like, maybe in her early thirties or so?" and I remember thinking, *Oh! That's the kind of woman I want to be when I grow up*. It was the first time I had seen an example of an adult woman I actually wanted to emulate. She was empowered, sensual, artistically brilliant, and gave no fucks. She was fierce and there was a resonance in my own being. She lit my pilot light.

What I didn't realize at the time: I was witnessing a queen.

She was sensual and sexual, but it wasn't coercive. This was not a display for us. This was an awareness and embodiment of herself that rose up through her experiences and became consciousness alive. Her material deals with sexual assault, misogyny, women's stories, and survival. Not only does she tell her own story, she also channels other women's stories into her art. Instead of veiling and hiding herself to survive, she was out there, waving her sensuality and living like a glorious warrior of light burning through all of our collective shame at once.

Watching Tori Amos performing for the first time—how she gave herself over the utter pleasure of what she was doing—expanded the picture of womanhood itself for me. Her shamelessness was implicit in her every move.

These are just a couple of the scenes that live in my *Book of Possibilities*. Sometimes just by being our silly, or free, or wild selves we become a part of other people's books. Even small moments like how you act at a birthday brunch.

It was my birthday and just for funsies I threw on a poofy princess headband that my friend Katy had given me the day before. An enormous bow made of sparkly silver and pink net attached to a pink plastic headband at a jaunty angle that gave it attitude—and that attitude was about to head bang to Madonna's *Lucky Star*. It was a birthday headband befitting a five-year-old girl that was also giving bachelorette party. It emanated the perfect balance of silly and cute—the kind you can get away with on your birthday.

This particular morning, I was having brunch with my girlfriend, Ellice, in Santa Cruz and the brunch place was packed. I got there before Ellice and put our name on the waitlist. She arrived and we were enjoying some good deep conversation on a little bench in the shade when the hostess called out what I had written on the signup list: "Holly Birthday! Party of two?" Then realizing what she was saying the hostess shouted out again, this time with extra cheer in her voice, "Holly *Birthday Girl*!"

I stood up and looked around the entire patio, enjoying the smiles of random strangers who saw my poofy headband and clocked that I was the aforementioned birthday girl. I leaned into the silliness of it all—a middle-aged woman in a princess headband announcing to the restaurant that it's her birthday—and with a huge grin, I said loud enough so everyone could hear, "Gee, I wonder why I wrote that down? Heh heh!" A group of older women knowingly chuckled, and as Ellice and I walked through the crowd towards the hostess, people started calling out, "Happy birthday, Holly!"

"Yeah, Happy Birthday!"

"Work it, queen!"

I paraded to my table through the cheers and applause that I hadn't enjoyed since I was marking birthdays in single digits. I may have even stopped and twerked a bit for the older ladies. There were high fives along the way. But you know what? It felt good. It felt fun! I had shamelessly enjoyed my birthday and drew others into the celebration.

These are the kind of shenanigans that I often get myself into. Not everyone wants that kind of attention from strangers, but I don't think of it as vying for attention so much as spreading an air of fun. Joy is just as contagious as shame, so why not spread more of it?

Stand-up comedy has helped to de-condition the Nice Girl. Taught me to say things and truly own them. It taught me the awful infectiousness of shame and yet also gave me the key to annihilating it and spreading joy instead. Most importantly, it has taught me to throw off the disguises and contortions and become a more honest version of myself. A funny thing happens when you no longer burden yourself with unnecessary shame. You are more likely to speak the truth. Which brings me to the next tenant of courage: honesty.

They say that the truth will set you free.

Well, not only that but it often makes for one helluva joke. So, without meaning to, without maybe even wanting to, through stand-up comedy I learned my own psychological weapon that no one sees coming. One that can heal rather than poison, even if it often pisses people off.

I learned to speak the truth.

CHAPTER VIII

Honesty: Killing It

*I'm practicing to be more honest and to not be
pressured into pleasing everyone all the time.
Sometimes when I go to get gas and the machine asks me
"Do I want a receipt? Yes or No?" I don't answer. I just leave!*

When a queen drops a truth bomb, it can be a powerful weapon. A sharp stick in the face of foggy facts and gaslighting. The truth is also a balm that we need to learn to use to heal the present. And lucky for me, it can also be hilarious. For example, the other night hosting a show:

"Hey, you people in the back, what are your names? You there, in the cap. Are you French?"

"No." He looked surprised but delighted to be included. He shrugged his shoulders and exchanged a look with his partner.

"Ok, well, French-cap guy, what is your name?"

"John," he said, with the obedience of a little boy answering a classroom roll call. Only I'm not as sweet as his third-grade teacher and I was just getting started....

"Hi, John, welcome. And what is the name of your date?" I gestured to the woman sitting next to him.

"This isn't my date." *Oh really?* I thought, *Okay then...* I pressed onward, not swayed just continuing my line of questioning, poking, curious, searching for the truth.

"Oh, okay, that isn't your date. Then who is it?"

"This is Brenda, my partner."

I can tell he meant partner as in romantic partner, but I took the opportunity to jab, "Brenda is your *business* partner?"

"No, my life partner," he responded, squeezing her in towards him in an affectionate way.

"Okay, so she's your life partner, but you aren't on a *date*?" I said simply pointing out the obvious. The audience laughs.

"Uh, yes," he answered somewhat sheepishly.

I paused for effect before I finally said, "I think that what he means, Brenda, is he ain't paying for dinner tonight," and with that the audience erupted into laughter.

It wasn't exactly comedy gold or anything revelatory, but it was funny because it was just an observation of what was happening. In comedy, sometimes simply repeating back what is said and stating the situation can be hilarious. And powerful. Truth telling is perhaps one of my favorite devices.

The Truth Can Kill

When a comedian has the audience in the palm of their hand, when they are making them scream with laughter, we often call that *killing*.[4] And nothing kills harder than honesty that is measured with great skill.

---

[4] Alternatively we might use the word *crushing*. I've always wondered, why do we use words that are so violent to animate success?

When I've worked with the LA comedian, Monique Marvez, I've often noticed her saying this, "I don't tell jokes, I just get up here and tell the truth." You know what? Her simply telling the truth is riveting. Her astute observations and ability to say what's in everyone's minds hits like a tornado of honesty, a stream of consciousness that's hilarious. It's hilarious because no one else will say it. But she gets up and articulates these things vividly with pointed imagery and shamelessness.

But you don't have to be as witty or as sharp as Monique Marvez. You can also just name what you see:

I do not think of myself as a naturally super witty person. Often (okay, this is embarrassing to admit), the times people are laughing at something I said was when I wasn't trying to be funny at all. As a result, when I'm on stage and doing any kind of crowd work or finding myself needing to deal with some situation in the audience I find the fastest way to funny arises not out of me *trying* to say something funny, but rather by just being super present in the moment and telling the truth. There are a few different ways that comedians use honesty.

Naming What's Happening

Narrate the situation. This can be a stalling tactic but it is also helpful to avoid misunderstanding and confront gaslighters. This is what I was doing in the example above with the French cap. I might repeat something someone said but slowly and with disbelief. Repeating his words back to him was enough to find the funny in the situation. These simple truths can be weirdly powerful and effective in crowd-work situations.

Another time I did this I was waiting in line for the bathroom before a show with another woman ahead of me. She was a pretty woman likely in her seventies, with white, cropped hair and a few tote bags on her arm. She reminded me of my own mom. We made small talk while we waited and then when it got to be her turn, she stepped into the bathroom, futzed with the buttons on the wall where the light switch would be, shrugged her shoulders, and went into the bathroom to pee in the dark. You had better believe this became a fun thing to bring up later when I was on stage.

"This lady right here, she couldn't even find the light switch in the bathroom! She peed in the dark!" The audience laughed knowingly. Many of them had futzed with the same bathroom light at some point that evening.

"Did you find the light switch?" the woman asked me from the audience. Her sincerity was the perfect levity for me.

"Yes," I answered confidently and the audience roared with laughter.

I leaned in and added another layer, "This woman peed in the dark! That is some skill." I mimed someone determinedly pulling their pants down. "*'I was a nurse in World War II, for crying out loud! I can pee in the dark!'*"

I mean sometimes the audience just feeds you the joke.

Stating the Obvious

Notice and put words to something so familiar we don't even see it anymore.

Maybe no one wants to say it, but more often no one thinks to point it out. Like in this joke I tell about tailgating:

> *My son invited me to his fraternity's tailgate party. I didn't even know what that was. It turns out it's when there's a game but you don't go…you just go right next to it. It's an event but you don't show up, but almost. I didn't know that was a tailgate party. I thought that was fatherhood.*

I'm considering something that everyone generally accepts and therefore doesn't necessarily think to question it. I'm stating the obvious about tailgating, but it's funny because it's a truth right in front of you that you didn't notice before.

Confessions

Share something that is secret and show your true feelings. The audience may or may not share them but they relate to the feeling of having secrets or private feelings they don't talk about. This is something I like to do a lot in the name of shamelessness. Like in this admission:

"You know, what I'm afraid of is the little crack between the wall and the stove where little pieces of food go to die. I never look back there. I've flipped whole pancakes in there."

Stretching the Truth

Tell a hyperbolic truth or an obvious lie to point to a greater truth.

I don't tend to use this device in comedy but some of the greats do. Consider this famous joke Steve Martin used to tell:

"I gave my cat a bath the other day… They love it. He sat there; he enjoyed it. It was fun for me. The fur stuck to my tongue, but other than that…"

We know this is a lie. Steve doesn't lick his cat, but it's true to the foolish character he was playing. It's also funny because we didn't see it coming. We hear he gave his cat a bath and we picture a cat immersed in water. Then he flips the image on us and that *comedic twist* surprises the laugh right out of us.

Elephant in the Room

Say the unsaid, the thing everyone sees but struggles to talk about. Speak a truth that no one wants to acknowledge.

Like the time I was talking to a couple in the audience that were a mixed interracial couple: She was White. He was Black. I didn't intend to mention anything about that. I asked them if they do each other's laundry (a typical question I ask because it leads to a joke about laundry) and the woman says she does the laundry because her husband doesn't separate the whites from the blacks. I told you. Sometimes the audience just hands it to you... So, then I named the elephant in the room by saying, "Yes I see that." The audience looked around at each other, mouths open in delight when they understood the double-meaning of the joke.

Being Honest with Yourself About How People See You

The best times are when you acknowledge something that's happening that everyone can see but most people wouldn't say. It can also be funny when you're honest about yourself. Knowing how the audience sees you can become a weapon. Like in the instance of my opener I mentioned earlier:

"My son is twenty-two... [I pause and look around at the audience as if searching for a certain reaction] All right, people are usually more surprised by that."

But Why is Honesty So Powerful?

Have you ever wondered why telling the truth is funny? Because it isn't always done. People lie more often than they tell the whole truth.

Sit with that one for a moment.

People lie more often than they tell the whole truth.

One of the reasons we lie is because in our culture we have put layer upon layer of restrictions on what we can and cannot say—what is appropriate and what is not appropriate. And comedy tends to circumvent all that. Human beings lie so often, through little white lies, intonation, encouragement, just to be "nice," and in all sorts of ways that when they actually say what is real, when we actually speak the truth, it strikes us as hilarious. Isn't that wild? And a little sad when you consider it—we're more accustomed to lying than truth telling—but the result is that because of its rarity we can use honesty as a weapon or a wand.

The Truth Can Be a Wand

I've always been fascinated with wands. Wave a wand around and make magic stuff happen. How dope is that? The truth can act like a wand: it's powerful and swift. The truth, like Glinda's wand from *The Wizard of Oz*, can transform you and heal you. It can send you back home. When cast about mindfully, the truth can change the course of events. It can even turn a toad into a prince... or a prince back into a frog.

I knew a woman who had a fun affair with another traveler while on a kibbutz. Afterwards he asked her if she would like to visit him a month later in Spain. For her it was a one-time deal and she wasn't so sure she wanted to continue the affair. But the guy was so into her and so convincing, to the point of buying her a plane ticket, she went against her gut and met him again. She ended up having a terrible time with him in Spain, not feeling the romance and recoiling from his advances until she met someone else. He was heartbroken and furious that he had spent so much time and money and energy on her; but if she had listened to her gut in the first place and spoken her truth she could have saved them both the misery.

Sometimes telling the truth is the kindest thing to do even if it is a difficult thing to do. It can save everyone time. A quick pinch earlier would have been kinder than refusing to speak the truth. Being honest with yourself when you feel like saying *no* or *yes* helps you not waste people's time. You are ultimately kinder that way.

The Truth Can Be a Weapon

Truth can be a wand of kindness and it can also be used as a weapon. There is power in naming what is happening or stating the obvious. This form of honesty is something to cultivate when stepping into your queen years. Stating the obvious disarms people who are trying to pull one over on you, it places the truth in the forefront, and it buys you time to think. Naming what is happening can be used in a myriad of ways:

- Dealing with gas lighters, manipulators and coercive people
- Restoring justice
- Deflecting projections
- Awakening people to their humanity
- Aiding in Nonviolent communication[5]
- Increasing shared understanding
- Decreasing miscommunication
- Holding people accountable
- Naming and dismantling assumptions

Like the time, many years ago, before I became a comedian, I confronted a guy who was trying to cut the line at the Cheeseboard. The Cheeseboard is a cozy employee-owned Bay-Area bakery in the heart of North Berkeley, a very liberal place; but also a place where the houses are either owned for generations by old-timer justice-fighting hippies, tenured professors from UC Berkeley, or affluent wealthy folks who can afford the adorable expensive houses in the area. Students, professors, affluent artists all pour into the Cheeseboard to get their fresh baked goodies often forming a line out the door and this day was no exception.

The way the Cheeseboard works is that the line winds around the perimeter of the inside, where there are glass cases filled with freshly baked goods. Most people wait to grab the items they want until they are at the point in the line where they are passing the baked goods.

---

[5] Non-violent Communication is a communication style that focuses on empathy and understanding to resolve conflicts. It's based on the principles of nonviolence and humanistic psychology.

CHAPTER VIII - HONESTY

On this particular day, I had been waiting in line for about 15 minutes, had finally gotten to the case of baked goods I wanted, and had just pulled out my asiago cheese bread when a short White man with glasses, about 65 years old, walks up out of nowhere and reaches around me to also grab some cheese bread. All fine and well, but when he was done reaching in the case, he just stood there directly in front of me, as though I didn't exist, as though he'd been in that line in front of me for 15 minutes. But he hadn't. He was—gasp!—cutting the line. My cheeky truth telling self wasn't going to let this go.

"Huh, okaaaay!" I said out loud to no one in particular. "That's interesting there, buddy!" My tone was light and jokey. "I guess you're just gonna get you your cheese bread and then stand in front of me like you've been here all along, mmm hmm."

The man's shoulders went very still, but he didn't turn around. He didn't say anything. This was the point where he could have turned around and realized his mistake or apologized. That's what I was prepared for. We'll laugh about it, I thought. But he didn't do that. He just continued to stand there directly in front of me and, honestly, too close to me. He was pretending like I didn't even exist.

Now I was starting to get pissed, so even though my tone was still teasing and light, there was a bite to it as I continued, "I guess we are just cutting the line then? That's what we're doing? Okay, I guess we all just cut the line whenever we want!"

The man turned around, angry. Being confronted with his own rude behavior provoked something from deep inside of him. "You are a sassy mouthed young lady!"

I was momentarily shocked. Shocked to be called a young lady and also reeling from the gall of this guy trying to turn it all around on me. "Excuse me?" I said in disbelief. "You're the one who cut me in line? There's this whole line of people and you just came in and grabbed your thing and cut right in front of me, sir." The word *sir* came out of my mouth like the sharp end of a shiv, jabbing at him with its insincerity.

He ignored the truth and continued, outraged, "You are a very rude, sassy mouth! How rude! You should be ashamed of yourself." *Check out this guy, lobbing that shame potato at me hard!* He was stammering with anger, his mouth and eyebrows furrowing and contorting with every word like they were trying to find a place to land.

"Oh ho! That's rich!" I laughed at the hypocrisy of the situation but I could feel the escalating rage of Earthquake Woman in my body. Wise Woman was nudging as well. I could tell this man's rage was going to evoke the rage in me and... all for what? A spot in line? *It's not worth it*, I decided in a moment. I took a deep breath and looked into this man's upset face. He was flushed bright pink and his glasses had slid down his nose a bit. *He's a boy in an old man's body, really. He's a little boy being called "bad."* The Wise Woman in me pulled in a touch of softness. "Listen," I say softly but directly, "You did cut in line, but I am going to just assume it was an honest mistake, okay? Let's just pretend like you didn't mean to do it. Let's just let it go, shall we?"

He was still spitting with rage. "Well, here!" He gestured dramatically and stepped behind me. "Please go ahead!" he said sarcastically.

"Thank you," I countered softly as I stepped in front of this man.

I stood there, trembling from the aftershocks of the encounter. My mouth tasted of sulfur and soot from extinguished flames. I felt the earth settling back into place. My nervous system was still alive and shivering and I tried to *breathe, breathe, breathe*. I could still feel this man seething behind me. And then just as I was trying to relax my stomach a bit, he started up again, still outraged and unable to hold it in. He was quieter, but nastier, too.

"You are a sassy mouth! Sassy mouth young woman."

His voice was inches away from my head. Wise Woman sighed. I sighed. I tried to remain calm but he continued. Taunting now. Determined to hurt me.

"So rude! You should be ashamed. You are a nasty woman. You should be ashamed of yourself!"

I shifted my weight from one foot to the other. *Calm calm calm.*

"Nasty woman. Shameful! Sassy mouth. You should be ashamed."

Out of nowhere, Earthquake Woman whirled around and threw my asiago cheese bread onto the floor at his feet. Something gooey and probably delicious shot out of the morsel and splashed onto his loafers. I barely noticed because simultaneously out of my mouth came, "You are nothing but a small, embarrassed man! Own your mistakes, motherfucker!" And with that I stormed out of the Cheeseboard empty handed. When I got into my car, I burst into tears, the Nice Girl in me taking it all on in a wash of embarrassment.

It sucked. I didn't want a huge confrontation. I didn't need that. But I couldn't let that injustice go. It was small and maybe down the line later in life I would learn to pick my battles better (an important queen lesson), but in this moment I was outraged that simply pointing out the truth had put me in the line of fire. Like Jack Nicolson in *A Few Good Men*, I wanted to roar, "You can't handle the truth!"

Later, as a comedian, I would learn skills that would have helped me in this situation. To keep it from escalating or simply to escape with my own center intact. But at this moment, I didn't have those skills yet. But I had learned a very important lesson about the truth: it can be very provocative.

The Truth Can Be Provocative

There is power in honesty mostly because it's rare. Or we use the truth in shady ways. Perhaps the truth is leverage to be used against someone, like a secret waiting to be revealed. Why do you think people gossip or have a hard time keeping a secret? The truth, when it comes out, is a real attention grabber. It thrusts the teller, however briefly, into the spotlight. Honesty is a secret weapon we all have access to, but are most afraid of using. Mostly because honesty has a big kickback. It doesn't always work out for the honest person. I've noticed this for a long time and it's the reason that comics can trigger people.

When I first got into comedy, I witnessed three physical attacks on comedians within the first year of doing comedy and that was a couple years before Will Smith smacked Chris Rock on stage at the Oscars. To attack a person onstage for… words. It's wild! I don't condone it, of course, but I can understand why it happens.

Honesty has one of two reactions. When a comic says something true that makes the audience feel "seen," they either laugh in surprise and recognition, or they feel shame and are activated.

Like I've said earlier, laughter in comedy is a door to let the shame out. It's a loophole in the societal structure. *That weird thing you thought nobody else does? Well guess what? You aren't the only one and here's the chance to laugh at it!*

That can be one reaction.

The other reaction is for the audience to feel attacked. And that comes from an unwillingness to let the shame out. It comes from an unwillingness to own your humanity and let yourself and everyone else off the hook.

The honesty in comedy is meant to help us to integrate the truth. We laugh, we put our hands together and clap.[6] But sometimes the audience isn't ready for it. Sometimes the charge they have around the topic you're joking about is too great and their anger too high. And sometimes when I'm walking around regular civilian life with my comedian brain in high gear, the general public isn't ready for it either.

CHAPTER VIII · HONESTY

I can't tell you how many times I've experienced a bit of a disconnect between worlds with my newfound comedian-style honesty. I'll be in the grind doing show after show and then I take a day or two off to attend a spiritual retreat or a dance intensive—both places and environments that I love, that nourish me, but also where people take themselves very seriously. The vibe isn't sarcastic, it's earnest.[7] I can't tell you how many times I've accidentally pushed buttons with some offhand jokes or remarks that to me are hilarious but to others wildly inappropriate.

On the one hand it can feel like these truths are just bursting inside of me, waiting to come out all of these years, but I realized I've been training for this truthfulness since I was 12 years old until now. My body and mind have forced a monthly reckoning on me and for years I hardly realized the value.

---

[6] I have this theory that clapping is helping to integrate our healing around certain subjects because it's bilateral stimulation and can act as a form of Eye Movement Desensitization and Reprocessing (EMDR), a psychological therapy modality that uses bilateral stimulation. Am I getting too woo woo? Am I whimsically forcing a structure of a clinical healing modality (EMDR) onto something that is just plain-old irreverent fun (comedy)? Yeah, maybe, but also, have we met?

[7] I find it interesting that in so-called spiritual or awakened environments my truth-telling can be so provocative. When we look to personal growth or spirituality, isn't the ultimate journey one towards exploring the truth? To me the highest form of spiritual awakening is to get in touch with the truth, the universal joke, and achieving a lightness of being that comes from a little irreverence.

The Contortion

You're a vault for so much truth that the CIA would pay you for your tips. Sometimes you feel like there are two realities: The one that is the truth and the one that everyone is pretending to be true. They are layered on top of each other and begin to blend in such a way that you start to wonder if you know what is the real truth after all. Going along with the game of pretend, you effectively gaslight yourself into believing the lies are real. Those times you do actually open your mouth and speak your truth you quickly follow it up with an apology because you're afraid you just hurt someone's feelings. This can sometimes piss people off even more. You aren't being real with them. They feel confused and unable to locate your true feelings. What follows is that you are also mad at yourself because you betrayed yourself with an apology you didn't want to make. Or perhaps you tell the truth and are punished for it, either by angering someone or retaliation. These kinds of responses to honesty train you to become silent, deceitful, sneaky, or shut down and detached from your own needs and desires. Meanwhile, the truth burns inside you, forging into something strong and solid, while you wait for the day when the timing is right and you can use this truth as a weapon.

The Great Reckonings of Truth: Menstruation and Perimenopause

Have you ever noticed when you get premenstrual, things feel a little harder? Things irritate you on another level and your threshold for dealing with other people's bullshit, deadlines, and traffic go way down? This is because your hormones that make you feel good drop down to an all-time low and you face the world as an exposed nerve. Earthquake Woman shifts the very insides of your womb and pinches you from the inside out, shaking pieces of you loose, leaving a bloody mess! For years I thought of these monthly reckonings almost as a disability, a hindrance to my fully energized and kindest, sweetest (read, nicest) self. The blood, the cramps, the irritability was something everyone made fun of with taunts of *Oooh a little bitchy; are you on your period? Hmmm?* Shove a bunch of Ibuprofen down your throat, grab a heating pad, and get to work. It felt like something to just bear down on and get through.

Until, I realized what was really happening during this time of the month. Until the wisdom of menstruation revealed itself. Now I like to view this irritability, this body's message to slow down, as a time of reckoning with the truth. As women, we aren't actually dealing with anything external that's different from the rest of the month. It's just that we have less resources to cope with things. The small things become big things. The truth reveals itself. And the same can be said for perimenopause and the queen years. When your hormones begin to change, you have less ability to ignore things that aren't working for you or sweep stuff under the rug. You need to have that tough conversation with a friend, or put your foot down with your boss about what you're able to accomplish. Your body is simply making it impossible to live in the lie that is our constant conditioning of pleasing people. You can't just stuff down your real emotions. The truth floats to the surface. Or should I say, roars?

It doesn't come nicely or quietly and definitely not politely. The truth has got all those layers of conditioning to fight through so she roars through us like an animal unleashed. She will not be silenced. She will not put up with crap. She will let herself be known. They say that when someone is stressed or in pain that is when you really see who they are. Any disguise they hold up can't withstand the pressure. The same is true for times of perimenopause. To pretend we are okay is dishonest. We are not ok. We are shedding our skin. We are ignited. We are becoming something greater than we were before!

Being dishonest is a disservice to myself. When we share truthfully (like I mentioned in the form of shamelessness and boldly asking for 100% of what we want) then at the very least we are less likely to be misunderstood and more likely to be seen authentically as we are.

I say this knowing it isn't always easy. I've had to try to learn to choose my moments. To be aware of how honesty will land in the spaces that I'm in. I learn from being onstage, feeling for the times in the room where the audience will allow me to kick open the door, and avoiding the tender places where I might say something that infuriates them. Sometimes I get it wrong. The only way to learn is to try and get it wrong a bunch until I figure it out.

Here are some things you can expect to be called when you start telling the truth: shit-stirrer, sassy mouth, provocateur, confrontational. People that are comfortable in the lies get really tense when someone wants to tell the truth. The interesting thing about my relationship with truth now is that it streamlines my life in some ways. It doesn't mean that other people like me more, but *I* like me more. But it's me or them and I don't want to have to trade my integrity for other people's comfort.

Like I said, there are two reactions to the truth in comedy: laughing and healing or shame and fury. Just like in life when we put ourselves out in the world and are bold, we can sometimes find ourselves in positions where we are vulnerable to threats. All of our fears can get triggered. But at some point, as we get into our queen years, we have just had enough of the hecklers and the bullies. We have to live in the truth because otherwise we are being disloyal to ourselves.

Chapter VII - Shamelessness

Fuck that.

Queen lesson number 245,575: Keep your eye on the prize... and the prize is you.

No one will be loyal to a queen who isn't first loyal to herself.

CHAPTER IX
Loyalty: Staying True to Yourself

Have you ever thought about the fact that a lot of wild shit goes down at slumber parties? From the seances, to the bras in the freezer, to the naughty confessions we murmured to each other whilst tucked inside our Rainbow Bright sleeping bags... slumber parties were a real delicious mess of vulnerability and kids' shenanigans.

I remember being at this one slumber party when I was in middle school. Through a 4H club in drama I had made friends with this one girl, Kelly, who went to Catholic school. She invited me to her slumber party with her Catholic school friends and then eventually I became friends with all of them and *voila!* I was inducted into a circuit of Catholic school girl slumber parties! All of a sudden, my weekends became full of them.

The Catholics, I discovered, threw great birthday parties and even better slumber parties. They put out good snacks, always ordered enough pizza, had nice carpet in their dens, and their parents often had Showtime and HBO, so we could stay up late watching movies with sex in them. I can't make these broad generalizations about all Catholics, but the Catholic middle-school girl parties I went to were the raunchiest. I remember one slumber party had an early co-ed portion of the evening. The birthday girl lined the boys up in the backyard with their backs pressed right up next to the house (where they couldn't be seen at a quick parent's glance) and us girls went down the line and kissed all the boys at the party one by one. We were 12 years old. It was wild times.

So, on this particular evening, I was at Trisha's slumber party. Trisha was the most petite 12-year-old I had ever seen, having retained her eight-year-old figure but still dressed like she was going to an Aerosmith concert: black leggings, high bangs, frosty pink lipstick. Her hair was so blonde it was almost white and it floated down her back like a cloud. Except for her adolescent acne, she looked like a perfect angel. An angel of rock 'n' roll. I was in awe of her. So me, Trisha and all these Catholic school girls decided to dress up, and lip sync in a pretend rock concert. As we rummaged around in Trisha's costume bin, I winced a bit to put on a miniskirt that the girls urged me to wear even though it barely covered my bottom. Already at 12, I was a few sizes bigger than everyone. Though still a girl myself, compared to the other girls, I was womanly and developed. I had hips and thighs, so nothing of Tiny Trisha's really fit me right. *Oh well*, I thought, affirming myself, *it's just gonna be us girls so who cares if it fits a bit scantily!* We got dressed up, turned on the music, and held her mother captive as our only audience. And I got into it. My tiny miniskirt outfit was wonky but, oh, I knew how to perform! I sang, I wiggled, I writhed sexily like I'd seen Madonna and Prince do. Me and my friends had a blast, but the exhilaration wasn't long lived.

A few days later I received a call from Trisha saying that her mom didn't want me coming over anymore and in fact she wasn't allowed to attend my own birthday slumber party, which was rapidly approaching in a few weeks. My friend was so upset about it she was crying and could barely get the words out. When I pressed her for details, she finally admitted that her mom had been shocked at seeing me dance around like that at her party and thought that I was *too sexual, too in my body,* and a *bad influence* on her daughter.

Talk about a transference of shame! I was heartbroken. Trisha cried as she told me and I cried as I took this in. And it felt unfair. How unfair to be cut out of the group for some perceived naughtiness that was really just a talented little girl expressing herself in an ill-fitting skirt. The real irony of this shaming and ultimately exclusion from the group was that I was the only girl in the group that weekend that had never even French kissed a boy! I was the least sexually experienced of the bunch and yet here I was being slut shamed!

But it didn't matter if I wasn't sexually experienced or not, because I had a womanly body and knew how to move sensuously, these were the messages I received. From church boyfriends to my friend's parents, to grown men, I was considered sexy and dangerous—even if I still played with Barbies and rode my bike around my neighborhood. Eventually I let the universe be my guide (I admit this wryly) and embraced it. If everyone said I was sexy, then I should see what that was about. And oh! Being a little seductress was exhilarating! Making older men squirm with embarrassed titillation when they found out how young I was. Garnering the attention, praise, desire of grown men—when had I ever been able to do that before? It was an easy slide from Nice Girl into a nasty one when no one was buying the nice-girl act anymore anyway!

Alas, this was just one more contortion. I contorted myself into something that I thought other people wanted from me just to get some of that sweet, sweet attention... even though that wasn't me. I wasn't sexually experienced. I wasn't interested in doing anything with these pervy grown men—gross! But the promise of attention, any attention, lured me in. Even though I got that attention that I wanted so badly, I was contorting. I was being disloyal to myself.

Then at some point in my thirties I realized these disloyalties were no longer serving me. It was hard to connect, it was hard to love, when I couldn't even locate where the love inside me was coming from. If I didn't know how to love and be loyal to myself then what did I have to offer anyone else? And then I embarked on the long journey of trying to peel these layers back. I tried to get to what was real, what was authentic to own my emotions, to feel them, to live in my truth. It was as if I had tried on so many layers of disguises in my youth only to spend the next 20 years trying to take them off. I did a lot of work. I went to a lot of workshops. I danced. I cried. I tried somatic therapy, EMDR, talk therapy, coloring vaginas in a yoni coloring book, reading selfhelp, going to seminars, workshops. *I pulled off so many layers, I wasn't even me. I was future me.*

Or so I thought. And then I became a comic. And I learned the hardest lesson, which is that comedy audiences see the truth pretty easily. Comedy audiences don't lie to you with their laughter. Or even if they try, it's pretty darn obvious when they're chuckling politely. Audiences are smart. They can feel when you're being disloyal with yourself. They can sniff it out.

Have you ever been in a situation where someone was lying to or trying to convince you of something but they were revealing little tells that indicated they weren't being completely honest? A salesperson, a poker game, your kid trying to get away with something. You might not be able to even name the tells in that moment, but you feel like something is off.

In comedy this happens as well. There are small drops in energy, or switches in tone that give you the information that something isn't right. Just like a football player who drops the ball, they aren't delivering on the joke. In these little moments we show audiences that we aren't fully confident in what we're saying. The words coming out of our mouth don't match our vibe. The audience feels it and it makes them tight or confused or both, which are bad for laughing.

Sometimes comedians will tell an obvious lie in order to get to the truth of something or to be funny. This is acceptable because through sarcasm or hyperbole the lie is clear to the audience. What the audience won't accept are the lies that exist inside the comedian themselves. These often come in the form of body language.

Telling a joke about being bold while shrinking backwards away from the audience. Sweating while trying to appear confident. Trying to do material that isn't in their voice. When your words don't align with your body the audience may not always be able to name it, but something feels off. That's why they will laugh often when a comedian who is having a bad set shrugs and says, "Well this is going poorly." It's a bit of a crutch and overused but they laugh because they can tell that at least the person is being honest. The words out of their mouth are congruent with what their energy and body are saying.

One of the hardest things I've had to learn in stand-up comedy is how to not just emit confidence, but to be 100% behind myself no matter if the audience is with me or not. To stand behind my material even when it isn't working. I would almost argue this is the *biggest* skill anyone has to develop to make stand-up comedy work. You have to learn how to not abandon yourself. No one wants to watch someone up there who doubts themselves. Sounds easy, right?

Well, it's easy in your head or at home when you're planning your material. *They'll definitely laugh here!* you think or, *Oh my god that is the funniest thing ever!* You chuckle naively to yourself. And then you get it in front of an audience and it doesn't go the way you want it to. No one laughs. It could be your delivery, or it could be something in the news that is on the minds of the people in the audience that day. It could actually be—and I'm not kidding here—the order of one or two words in the punch line! For whatever reason, the joke doesn't work and you have two choices. You can let it throw you off course or you can just continue on like nothing is wrong and rework the bit later.

I'm in favor of that latter approach. There are some exceptions where it is better to acknowledge that it didn't work with the audience with an admission like, *Oh wow, y'all hated that, huh?* But you can even do that in a way that still doesn't abandon yourself.

Now being loyal to yourself doesn't mean you're not open to feedback when something isn't working. Self-loyalty doesn't equate to stubbornness or an unwillingness to acknowledge areas of improvement. You can still be loyal and listen to whether the audience is laughing or not. You can still stick with yourself while reworking or discarding a joke. It's not about your precious material; it's about not abandoning yourself. Just because a joke isn't worthy doesn't mean that you're not. It's a beautiful balance—self loyalty. You are essentially saying, *I'm with her* and at the same time being open to the idea that she can make mistakes.

How We Abandon Ourselves

Comics find so many different ways to abandon themselves onstage: Saying "I don't know" over and over in between jokes, panicking or rushing, abandoning their material and pandering to what they think the audience wants (there's a fine line between pandering and pivoting that we'll talk about later). They're ghosting their own goals, undermining themselves by pressing the well-this-isn't-going-well button too often, and by becoming disinterested in what they're saying.

And it isn't just comics. We all do these things that undermine and abandon ourselves. How often have you…?

- Apologized when you didn't need to
- Didn't ask for something you really wanted

CHAPTER IX - LOYALTY

- Were offered what you wanted and turned it down
- Disparaged yourself when someone gives you a compliment
- Trailed off in the middle of a sentence...

It's so frustrating, but I've done all of these things so many times. I remember years ago getting really worked up by a work dynamic. I was on a team that kept failing to recognize my strengths and my contributions. Every time I attended a meeting and it came time to figure out the action items, I felt undermined by a few of the team members who would say stuff like, "Oh Holly can take that." I kept getting stuck with admin items instead of the juicy creative stuff that I was really wanting to do more of.

Instead of saying something in that moment, I told myself I would just get overwhelmed with disappointment and when pressed for an answer would find myself saying, "Okay, no problem!" cheerfully as though I were someone else. Later on I would complain to my sister on the phone about it and my Earthquake-Womanly anger would rise to the surface as I spoke about it: "No one is letting me do what I want! Why don't they see me?! It's infuriating!"

What I failed to recognize at the time, was that I wasn't actually mad at my teammates. The irritation came from not being loyal to myself. By saying, "Okay, no problem!" I was betraying my own desires to please someone else. There we go with the Nice Girl behavior once again! But the anger was coming up because my actions were personally disloyal.

When we go along with other people when we secretly don't agree we get angry and frustrated because we are being disingenuous. It is a soul splitting activity. Our soul is guiding us one way, while our actions are pushing against it and doing something else. It's infuriating because it makes us feel invisible and turns us away from the attention we might like to receive. Abandoning yourself is like turning the lights out on your house on Halloween while you sit in the dark with a bowl of candy and feel sad no one is knocking on the door. Nobody is coming by. You've made yourself invisible. You've announced nothing worth seeing here. You've shut off the lights at your own show.

So, how do we become more loyal to ourselves? What are some ways you can start exercising this muscle even if you're not a stand-up comic? Once again, the answer can be found in art. Building trust with yourself is just the same as building it with an audience. Continuity matters. Sustainment matters. Paying attention to those moments in between a question and an answer.

> ### The Contortion
>
> You crack the meanest jokes on yourself. People around you might laugh at your self-effacement, but it only diminishes how the world sees you. You try to backtrack and offer something else only to abandon it immediately when it doesn't land and then you get angry, bitter, and your self-esteem goes way down. You wonder why no one will listen to what you say! You lurch the other way: start doing wild things to show everyone how confident you are. To grab attention. You are desperately seeking approval from everyone else because you don't feel it in yourself. You are testing your friends and silently counting and admonishing the ways they show up or don't because you are craving a loyalty that you are refusing to give to yourself.

CHAPTER IX - LOYALTY

The Art of Staying Loyal to Yourself

As a comedian, when I submit an audition tape pretty much any booker who knows what they're doing will ask me to provide a continuous clip, meaning there are no edits from one joke to the next. No one has ever said why they ask for this but I think it is partly to make sure they can see how the audience reacts and partly because the real professionalism shows not just in the jokes themselves but in the moments between the jokes. How do you carry yourself from one moment to the next? How do you hold the tension, stay with the audience, react or pivot, and be present in the moment? How does the comic handle it when the audience doesn't laugh? Do they move forward and try to get them back or do they abandon themselves? It's in those places between jokes where the amateur will drop their connection with the crowd, look down, or fidget uncomfortably and "show the seams" of the performance. They'll let you know they're thinking of the next bit they want to perform. They drop the curtain. The professional know-how to sustain the act even when they're not talking.

I love performing stand-up comedy. It's what I want to do most of the time. But just like anyone, occasionally I have off nights where I'm feeling off, vulnerable, weepy, a little less than confident, and I just want to crawl under my electric blanket instead of getting on stage and being judged by people. I always stay and finish the show. But before I take the stage, I find a way to get in alignment with it. Or in acceptance of where I am. I don't just put a smile on. I try to line up with my truth for that night and do the jokes from there. I've found that this is the best solution. Better than trying to muster up more enthusiasm. The audience will be more forgiving if you are honest with them, if you are honest and loyal to yourself. They won't forgive you if you appear fake. If you have integrity, if you are fully living with the truth of who you are in that moment, then the audience resonates with that and my jokes are more powerful. No one sees the tells in between the jokes or the drops in energy because they don't exist. Or if they do, you name them, you tell the truth. You stay true to yourself.

In comedy, these transitions, maintaining this consistency, is vital to a performance; so, what about the transition into our queen years? Queens, we are at a time where we can feel where the seams are. We feel when we break the moment, the friendship, or we drop the ball but also we are beginning to care less. We're exhausted from smoothing everything out for everyone. Here's the magic trick. Keep your eye on the prize: Yourself. If we stay loyal to ourselves, and allow ourselves to be honest, in a way we are doing everyone a favor, there are less cracks in the seams. Even if we're an angry ball of hormonal imbalance, at least we're consistent in some ways. At least people can gauge what kind of person they're dealing with.

This can also cause friction. Those people who were used to us picking up the pieces and shaping them nicely together are shocked by our sudden abandonment. You choose working out over being at home when your partner gets home. You choose a morning writing practice over making lunch for your loved one. You leave a party abruptly and without apology because you know you'll feel better when you go to bed by 11:00pm. Gone are the days of constantly bending to everyone else's needs. Self-loyalty means learning to set and keep boundaries.

Boundaries

When it comes to boundaries, I have come across so many teachers... by teachers, I mean people who have pushed my boundaries. Make no mistake, these annoying people are really the only people who can teach you and make you realize

1. *Aha! I have a boundary!*
2. *I know that now because you crossed it.*

3. *I don't like this and I have to do something or you'll drive me nuts!*

Here are some of my best boundary teachers:

The client who wouldn't take no for an answer when she wanted to force her Hollywood actor friends to do hypnotherapy sessions with me even though they didn't want to and I had to tell her that I don't take clients that way.

All of the bookers who wanted me to take the gig for less. Or when I simply ask for the details of the gig, they tell me the venue and time, but not how much money, so it's like pulling teeth to extract the info out of them.

Being expected to take notes at a meeting just because I was the only woman present.

The boss who texted me on my personal phone and got angry when I didn't help him with his taxes after I had already stopped working at the company.

The director who used to cancel rehearsals at the last minute all the time, expecting me to rearrange my life to make it work for them.

Lots of annoying people! I've had lots of boundary teachers!

When you encounter these boundary teachers and begin putting your foot down, it isn't easy at first. Especially if you are setting a new boundary with someone who is used to pushing them.[8] Other people may feel hurt or shut out or let down. I would argue that you aren't just dropping the ball... you are changing people's expectations entirely.

---

[8] I've found it's always easier to set boundaries in the beginning rather than later on in any kind of relationship.

You are creating a new narrative and it isn't that you can't be trusted, it's just that those things that can be counted on are different. You are redefining your boundaries: You may not respond to texts immediately, but you create the expectation that you will at some point respond in the next 48 hours. You may not be available for everything your friend wants you to do, but you create the expectation that you will be honest about what actually feels good to you and honor your own needs.

Basically, when a woman enters this time of life, they drop the show for others that is making everything okay and all right all the time and they enter the greatest most authentic performance of their lives. One where their first loyalty is to themselves. And once everyone catches up to this new style and its rules of play, things will smooth out once again.

How to Stay Loyal to Yourself When It's Difficult

It happens more than I would like to admit. I'm up there on stage having a grand ol' time of it and for some reason it's not landing. This can result in a couple of different things. The audience is not laughing, but they're listening. Or, worst case scenario they are talking over me. They take their attention away.

It's one thing to change someone's mind when they're listening. Attention is like a string with each person in the interaction holding one end of it. If someone's paying attention to you, then at the very least you can tug on the chord and they'll feel it. It's harder when you're ignored completely. There's no cord. You have to find a way to reattach it. Cast it back out to the person you're trying to engage, not unlike a fishing line. An amateur might want to wave their arms, shout, get wilder, or do any variety of flashy things to get attention. It's comparable to a young girl flashing her tits for attention. We don't need to go there. It's a bit humiliating and self-abandoning.[9] Here's an example of how I stayed loyal to myself and got the attention back.

I was doing a bar show the other night. Cute little stage, little noisy, but not a bad spot. For whatever reason this night was not the best audience. There were maybe 10 people that were there to listen to the comedy. And that's what they were doing for every comic. Just sitting and listening as though they were watching TV. Every comic took the mic and performed for silence, so before I even got up there, I knew it was going to be rough.

Finally it was my turn and I got up there. Some of my tried-and-true jokes got some laughs; but there were a lot of things that played to silence, or near silence. I thought I could hear a chuckle here or there. I didn't want to disconnect from the audience but I couldn't really hear their response. And I felt the back of my neck get hot and damp with sweat. I felt this urge to speed up. My inner critic shouted, *Okay, they don't like it. I should just do my stuff fast and get outa here!* But underneath the critic, there was also another impulse and this one was saying *Make them listen to you! Make them listen! I will force them to laugh with my clownish antics!*

I felt all this come up as a wave of strong urges, but instead of giving into them, I just let them be there. I took a breath and grounded myself. Felt my feet on the floor. Felt the sensation of my hips. And I let myself take my time. I did my jokes and I turned my attention inwards to listen more to what I was saying so that I started getting pleasure from my own words. Instead of trying to drag something out of them, I tried to enjoy myself the best I could.

I didn't disconnect from them either. I didn't think *fuck you* or overreact. I decided to have a good time regardless. This isn't a story

---

[9] Or is it? My mind goes to comedian Chelsea Handler who's been known to ski down a hill topless for social media just because she can. Just because it's funny. I guess it's all in the spirit with which you flash your titties. Please, don't use my opinion as a rule. Flash whatever you feel like.

about me popping the room, but I got through it. I stayed loyal to myself and had a good time and preserved my loyalty to myself no matter what happened around me.

Emotional Fluency

This is an example of a time I was able to regulate my own emotions. It was not a life-threatening scenario, but the less risky situations can be the best times to practice emotional fluency. Recognizing the signals from my body that are telling me I want to speed up, go harder, and be louder out of desperation—this is emotional fluency. Being able to feel the emotions of embarrassment rising to the surface and to just let them be there—this is emotional fluency. Finally, to feel all the things, but to still gently refocus myself back onto my own pleasure or my innate sense of wellness—this is emotional fluency. Not only have I learned the language of my own feelings and the body signals they produce, but I'm also able to speak it fluently back to them when I need to.

Has something similar ever happened to you? Maybe a family member started criticizing you and you didn't take the bait, understood the feelings coming up for you in the moment and navigated that conversation gracefully without losing yourself? Maybe you had an encounter with a frenemy who was trying to manipulate you and you were able to stop and see things clearly.

Emotional fluency is knowing that no matter what emotions or fears come up you will be able to handle it. You will be okay. You learn how to understand those emotions more quickly and redirect them, soothe them, or direct their power without feeling used by them. Because when you have that kind of emotional fluency, you can face anything.

We can't change what happens around us or to us, but we can control our reaction to it. And sometimes if we're lucky, these conscious empowered actions send waves out around us and can help to change others as well. But we can't count on that. All we can control is our response. Our own healing. Safeguard ourselves by becoming emotionally fluent and learning to lovingly work with our own fight-or-flight responses.

Our queen years are a time of reckoning and reality. We cannot control the outside world, but we have been learning and collecting data about ourselves which we can control. We've been the researchers of our own emotional tides and now is the time to figure out what works for us and how we manage it because the alternative is dire. We cannot live in constant stress, fear, and anxiety. It affects every aspect of our health.

In case you haven't been introduced to the science behind our fight-or-flight response, let me break it down for you. Your body produces two hormones under stress—adrenaline and cortisol. They are also known as your *flight-or-flight* hormones. Produced in the adrenal glands, adrenaline increases your heart rate, blood pressure and boosts energy, while cortisol increases blood sugar levels. This is meant to protect you when there is the threat of attack. Your body is all charged up and ready to run, fight, or even freeze to keep you safe.

However, you should know that cortisol also alters your immune system responses and suppresses the digestive and reproductive systems. Once the stress passes, your hormone levels drop, and your body should return to its normal state; but long-term (chronic) stress can disrupt almost all of your body's processes. Anxiety, high-sugar diets, and conflicts at home or work can lead to the adrenal glands sustaining high levels of cortisol, which can lead to depression, exhaustion, headaches, insomnia and brain fog.

The fact of the matter is, due to the variety of stressors in our lives, we don't always return to a normal state. This is why it is all the more important to learn how to recognize and regulate our bodies and minds. I like to think of it as lovingly befriending my fight-or-flight response. By directing our minds, we can not only get better at regulating ourselves back to a more relaxed state when any threat has passed, but we can actually use these responses, the energy that adrenaline brings as they are intended—to fight or get the heck out of a situation—essentially to keep ourselves safe.

As a hypnotherapist and someone who has been studying the effects of stage fright for years for myself and my clients, I have a lot of practice and tools at my disposal for using this fear response when it comes up; but it's something anyone can learn. Whether you spend time on stage or not, unless you are living in a cave you encounter triggering experiences that provoke your body into a heightened state that is useful, but if left unchecked, can be potentially harmful. All that extra cortisol in your body can lead to auto-immune diseases, heart conditions, weight gain and more.

As queens we have to learn how to use our fight, flight or freeze responses in the moment instead of feeling hijacked by them. We have to assume that maybe our bodies know something we don't and become a partner to our responses learning how to run it rather than it running you. There's a reason we avoid doing the work to get good at this.

Avoiding the Hard Feelings

Think about all the things I'm asking you to do in this book:

Love yourself no matter what! Don't give up! Be shameless! Be bold! Ask for what you want! And be honest! By goddess, speak truth to power!

Doesn't it all sound so familiar? It's probably nothing you haven't heard before, so why is it so hard to *do*?

Women aren't *not* doing these things because we don't know we should be, or because we don't want to. Everyone wants to love themselves, feel confident, be able to speak openly and pursue what they want in life. We don't do them because we are *avoiding the feelings* that go along with these actions if it doesn't go well. We are avoiding disappointment, embarrassment, shame, and potential humiliation. We are avoiding those feelings and the sensations they leave in our bodies.

But what if we didn't have to avoid those feelings? What if we were comfortable with being more, well, uncomfortable? Our biggest holdback is that we are often not emotionally fluent. We are unskilled at having emotions that we don't enjoy like sadness, anger, and disappointment. If we want to be bold, confident, and shameless, we can't just pretend we don't care. We can't just pretend or suppress the emotional byproducts of taking bigger swings in life. We have to actually take the reins on those emotions that happen when we do care. We need to become emotionally fluent in our own languages of fight-or-flight so that we can become emotionally resilient.

Even though we like to joke among us that comedians are soulless, becoming a stand-up comedian hasn't safeguarded me from having feelings. It has actually done the opposite. It puts me in the middle of them again and again. Forces me to know the fear when it comes up, feel the humiliation and the shame when it gets hurled in my direction, and to really speak with it. To dialogue with it, to live with it night after night on stage. When you talk daily to the emotions of your soul, eventually you begin to understand them. You speak their language. You know how to be partners with them instead of fighting with them.

The world is full of hecklers, people and things to provoke the hell out of us. That's not going away. So, our courage can't be something we just know on an intellectual level. It has to be a familiarity with these parts of ourselves. The real test of courage isn't about becoming immune to these emotions like fear, it's about whether we can be courageous along with them. If we wall ourselves off from feeling, that is inhumanity; but to become partners with our emotions allows us to take bigger risks while also maintaining our empathy for ourselves and others.

How do you gain that emotional fluency, though? Where does that resilience come from? Sometimes you have to be tested, in all different ways, in order to gain this skill. And no one tests you better than a heckler. And, oh boy, have I been tested! Like this one time I faced a man-bear in a bar…

CHAPTER X

All Your Courage: Dealing with Hecklers

I don't mind getting older... I still feel vital, attractive, but there are certain things I miss. Like the other day I walked past an unmarked white van and had this thought... Aww, no one is trying to drag me into a white van anymore.

I had just come from an LGBTQ+ open mic. It was at the White Horse Bar in Oakland, a notoriously queer bar and this particular open mic that night run by my friend Tanna was the kick-off for pride month. Queer spaces tend to be more inviting and accepting with less of a bro vibe in general. Even just the straight men that do show up tend to be more respectful so I was feeling all safe and warm and fuzzy coming from the queer space. Then I decided to try and hit another open mic. This one was run by a guy in a bar in Point Richmond. I'd been there before and it wasn't unwelcoming in any way, it was just more locals, more tradesmen showed up. Regular folks from this small industrial beach town.

I started off my set with the most innocuous of jokes, "I'm a parent. Anyone else have the soul sucked out of them?"

A burly man near the front of the stage raised his hand in answer to my question. His face was an angry red, like it had been tortured by hours in the sun and his clothes were a workman's clothes: distressed layers of denim, plaid and canvas ending in huge boots at his feet. The hand that he raised was so big and swollen with hard work, it looked like a paw. He had the look of a weathered sailor: Large. Muscled. Very drunk. "Oof yeah," I said in response to his raised hand. "Having kids is rough."

"Actually," he says very loudly. "I love being a dad! I have five kids and wish I had one hundred." His tone is aggressive like he's got something to prove.

"Aw that's nice, but that ends the audience participation portion of the evening," I said cheerfully, except I didn't get all of that out before he said it again, this time even louder and with menace.

"I'm a great dad!"

Now I could tell he was one of those men who thinks he's got to become part of the show and that I'd need to start shutting him down if I had any chance of trying out my new material, so I veered towards the truth. I named what was true in the moment in an attempt to disarm him. "Yeah, okay, sure, you're a great dad but uhhh you are here... on a Monday night... So how great of a dad are you then?" A simple jab. Sharp and hurtful sure, but usually effective at shutting someone up so we can laugh and move on.

These moments with a rowdy audience member are like playing speed chess. Fast moves. One after the other. Moving somewhat intuitively:

I'll meet your *I'm a great dad* with the truth: *You are in a bar on a school night.*

CHAPTER X · ALL YOUR COURAGE

But he was talking over me so I went, "What?"

He shouted, "You better shut the fuck up about my kids!"

Whoa.

At first, I was baffled. I was thinking to myself like *I don't know your life, Popeye, why you got your panties in a bunch?* and then he repeated it, "You had better. Shut. The fuck. Up! About my kids!" and it was as though I had awakened some ferocious bear that had been sleeping inside of him. "Don't talk about my kids!" He half rose out of his chair like he was going to charge the stage. Like he couldn't wait to.

The threat hung in the air. I looked at the rest of the audience. Everyone was silent. He was the closest person to me and only a few feet away from the stage.

All of a sudden, I wasn't at a comedy show. I was in a boxing ring. It wasn't fun. It was threatening.

It's moments like these when I've realized it isn't enough to cultivate these muscles of courage: loyalty, shamelessness, honesty, boldness and persistence. I also have to be ready for what happens when I use these muscles.

Because what I've discovered is that when I stand in a place of self-love, brazenness, truth, asking, and determination, I can provoke some pretty big reactions in people. I can awaken the sleeping bear inside them. Which brings me back to the warrior aspect of stand-up comedy: dealing with the hecklers.

A World Full of Hecklers

A comedian's biggest teachers are the attention givers, the regular audience members but also the hecklers themselves. The greater audience is filled with people who understand that this is a comedy show and that they are the audience. They are there to be entertained and understand that for the most part their job is just to listen, laugh, and enjoy. No extra participation required or desired.

But then there are the hecklers. These are people who for whatever reason can't seem to keep themselves from participating, interrupting, or being downright rude. Not all hecklers mean to be a nuisance. Sometimes they can't help themselves from blurting something out, or don't realize that talking to their friend during your set is an interruption. Part of the magic of stand-up comedy is making it appear like we are just having a conversation with the audience. Add alcohol to this situation and people can forget where they are and start talking back or cheering too loudly or… any number of little heckles. We learn to deal pretty swiftly with all of these and more, but when someone is negating all of my hard work by their interruptions and throwing me off my rhythm, I can't help but break out of character to handle it. There have even been times when Earthquake Woman has shut that shit down by telling them to *shut the fuck up* or something even meaner. Those times are the real pain-in-the ass heckling. The kind that makes you lose your cool.

When I talk to women in the audience after a show the number one thing I hear most of them say is, *I could never do that*, meaning stand up. But, honey, in a way you already do. The world heckles you all the time. And it's not easy being a human on this planet let alone a human woman.

Stand-up comedians aren't the only ones to deal with hecklers. The world is full of hecklers. Hecklers show up in regular life as the guy who stares at you too long, the one who overshares or over-explains or gives you unsolicited advice when you're in the middle of a sentence. It can be done innocently, like the coworker who thinks you are not getting your point across so they interrupt because they think they're helping. Or it can be done not so innocently, like in the case of a bully.

Stand-up comics get heckled so regularly that we learn how to manage this sometimes unconsciously. I was never good at this before I

CHAPTER X - ALL YOUR COURAGE

was a comic. Faced with a bully in real life I would get flustered, run and hide, or turn on myself and feel like I'd done something wrong to cause the conflict. I can't say that happens so much anymore. Stand-up comedy has taught me how to stand up to bullies and stay in integrity.

No comics really love this unless they're 100% crowd-work comics but we all have to deal with it, so we all learn how to deal with it. Effectively. Hopefully.

"I'm Just Trying to Help."

When I first started taking the stage as a comedian, I often came up against what I like to refer to as the person who thinks they're helping. I know you're thinking this must be a man, but surprisingly I've been heckled by people of every gender, though I must say it is more infuriating when it comes from a man.

Like the one time I was on a show only six weeks into my comedy career and a guy in the front row interjected. An older Black gentleman with glasses, about 60 years old, wearing grey slacks and a cardigan. He had been leaning back in his chair the entire show with a kind of unconvinced attitude. He had been silent for everyone else, but when I got on stage, he suddenly became animated and didn't hesitate to interject after one of my jokes, "You know what else is funny...."

I tried to shut him down. "No, sir, this isn't about you."

"But that same thing happened to me and I gotta tell you...."

"Oh, okay." I threw up my hands. "I guess this is just a conversation between you and me now!" The audience laughed as I playfully rested my bottom on the front of his table and leaned towards him dramatically like we're best friends.

The guy didn't get that I was joking, however, and instead saw it as an invitation to just keep going. Finally, I cut him off, "Please, sir, I'm trying to do my stuff."

"I know. I'm trying to help you...."

I looked to the producer, but he didn't appear to be moving in to help anytime soon. He just watched it all go down unfazed.

I had the microphone in my hand. I was louder than this guy, but the room was small so everyone could hear him. I felt utterly thrown off by this insistent interruption because, remember, I was only a few weeks in and hadn't learned how to manage these kinds of folks. I struggled for another minute or so trying to continue with his constant interruptions. Then I got the light, which means the producer in the back of the room was waving their phone light around to let me know my time was up. Frustrated, I finished my set and sat down, defeated by this heckler.

I'm trying to help you....

There's a reason I don't get as many of these types of hecklers anymore. My confidence and skill have improved. This man was probably sincerely moved by my newbie lack of confidence and did want to help me. It was the wrong move, but how can we expect any less when we treat women in our society as though they are helpless, incompetent, and in need of constant assistance?

How often do women experience guys like this, who offer assistance when it isn't warranted or needed, but rather comes off as condescending? Forget about opening doors, fellas. Open any fucking door for me that you want. If you're right behind me, I'm going to open a door for you, too. I really like some regular human helpful offers of assistance when I need them. I'm down with that. But I don't like when someone sees me in a powerful position and assumes I can't get the job done. I don't like it when it's clear they think I'm going to need help leading a team and so they undermine my authority. Any woman can relate to this feeling. *Back off, I've got this!* And if we don't it's because we haven't had the practice, due to removal from leadership and powerful positions!

CHAPTER X - ALL YOUR COURAGE

Attention is kind of like having the talking stick! There are those people who can't go long without it and will do anything to yank the attention back on themselves.

Sarah Silverman says it best:

> A lot of people heckle, and they're well meaning. Hecklers fascinate me because, whatever the words they're saying, the subtext always is "I exist!" And to me it's heartbreaking and fascinating and I want to give them what they want.

The helpful heckler at the show that night may have thought he was swooping in to assist, but on another level all hecklers are trying to grab attention.

Courage in the Face of Men and Bears

You know that social media meme that made waves in 2024 about meeting a bear or a man in the woods? So many men were in an uproar because when faced with the question, "Would I rather be stuck alone in the woods with a man or a bear?" Most women chose the bear, our reasoning being that the bear is just trying to survive. Yeah, it could kill you, but the bear doesn't have a fragile ego you have to tiptoe around or malicious intentions. When women answered that we'd rather be faced with a bear what we were pointing to was the wisdom that we have been gleaning for decades, probably even centuries, without ever explicitly saying which is this: Inside every man there is a ferocious bear, but there isn't a fragile masculine ego inside every bear.

This is the kind of fragile ego I've learned to identify as potentially dangerous. It may seem overly cautious to say I was afraid that man would attack me in the bar that night in Point Richmond, but statistically it's not.

Nearly 89,000 women and girls were intentionally killed worldwide in 2022, (according to data from the United Nations.) One-in-three women across the globe have experienced intimate-partner violence or non-partner sexual violence. One in three. Now add to those odds a woman who is out in bars and clubs four-to-six nights a week saying some sassy provocative-ass shit into a microphone and I've just made myself a target. I get that it's risky so I try to use all my spidey senses and queen experience to deal with situations before they can escalate.

So back to that night at the open mic where the truth had sent this man into unreasonable fury: What had happened was that I had awoken the ferocious bear inside the man. It was as though I was a thorn that the bear had stepped on and now the bear was yelling at the thorn:

"Shut the fuck up!" he barked. Just his very energy and tone of voice threatened violence.

I paused, frozen. I shook my head a bit in disbelief. He had the gall to talk while I was trying to do my set, so I made a harmless joke and now I had to stand here and have my physical being threatened?

There were *so* many ways I wanted to humiliate this man. The Comedian in me was dying to ask him if he'd had his nap today because he seemed a little grumpy. Wise Woman wanted to explain what was happening, "*Sir, you have been activated because you are feeling insecure about your role as a father in your children's lives. I'm sorry to be the one to hold up a mirror to you, but it's not me you're mad at, it's yourself.*"

Earthquake Woman was dying to call his bluff. "*You need to sit down. Stop trying to intimidate a woman and shut the fuck up.*" But I didn't say any of these things.

All of the hundreds of times I've gone on stage and had people heckle me have made me an expert in dealing with interruptions. Over the years I've been doing stand-up comedy, I've learned many ways to deal with these situations and stay on course in my set. I have done it all, but nothing took my power away faster in that moment than feeling like I was being physically threatened by a man twice my size. So, I was pissed. I was pissed at him for taking away my power.

I couldn't make myself speak. I was frozen. I did turn my head away from him and look out towards the back of the room. At least I could do that. By taking my eyes off of him, I took my attention away. I was trembling. Too pissed to sit down. *I won't let that fucker win.* But my nervous system had been hijacked and I couldn't say anything.

He repeated, "You don't talk about my kids. You shut the fuck up!"

No one in the place moved a muscle. I realized I still had the microphone, so I asked for what I needed. "Can I get someone?" My voice was trembling. I looked for the host and continued, "Can I get someone to come closer to the stage with me?" A large man, a comic from earlier, came up to the stage, but before I could give him further instructions, he tried to take the microphone out of my hands so he could say something to the guy. "No, that's not what I need," I said, exasperated. "Get out of here. C'mon. Thank you, but no." I shooed him away.

At this point the host was making his way towards the stage and I said, "Yes, Tom, thank you. Can you just… uh." He jumped on stage and yelled, "Give it up for Holly!" It was weird but he was trying to rally support for me in this awkward way. "Thank you, Tom. Can you just sit on that chair, please, while I do my set?" He took a seat on the chair that was on the side of the stage.

"Thanks. Okay…" I felt a little better with him sitting up there with me but I was still frozen. I tried to venture to my next joke. "My boobs are trying to get a divorce." Here I was with this big scary man staring daggers at me and I decided to talk about… my tits. I felt like a cartoon of myself.

Tom laughed way too loud trying to be supportive but the rest of the room wasn't buying it. We were all still shaken, navigating the cold freeze this man's presence had put on the room.

I was still shaking with fear. My animal body could not release the threat of this drunken angry man glaring at me in the shadows only a few feet away. My breathing was hard and shaky like I had just hiked to the top of a large hill with no stopping. It made an awkward whooshing sound into the microphone, exactly the type of sound you're supposed to avoid in stand-up comedy. It means your mic is too close to your mouth. Only I couldn't pull the mic away, my arm was trembling and I couldn't remember how to move it. I breathed and shook and tried to get it together for way longer than anyone was comfortable with. But I did not want to let that man win... and finally that man got up and slinked out of the room. As soon as he left, I let out a big breath.

I said to the sparse room of onlookers and a few comics, "Wow, I just. You know? I drove all this way. So, if you don't mind, I'd really like to talk about my titties just a little bit more. Is that okay?"

"Yes!" There were some supportive noises and some smattering of applause. There were not that many people in the audience really to muster much more than that.

So, I told my jokes as best as I could. It didn't go great, but it didn't go badly either, all things considered. When I finally came off stage I immediately burst into tears. Another female comic hugged me and suddenly I was surrounded by the bartender and staff, who offered support and told me they had made the man leave the bar entirely.

Later, I debriefed with my sister and she pointed out I did the best thing. "You didn't fight him because we all know he would have attacked you. You didn't flee because then he wins and fuck that, but you froze. Actually, you could look at it another way. You really stared him down."

"Wow, you're right. I met a man in the woods and I stared him down."

Using All Your Courage

When we're really out there using our courage, we don't always get to win the way that we want. We might not knock out the bad guy or get to wave our glorious flag in the air, but we can often win quietly. By standing

CHAPTER X - ALL YOUR COURAGE

there that night and just breathing, not backing down, but not breaking the tension of silence either, I gently let the air out of his balloon, letting it seep out slowly instead of popping it. Either I made him sheepishly realize that he was being a dick or he just got bored and crept away. Doesn't actually matter. Either way I stared down a bully.

In hindsight I used all five muscles of courage:

Loyalty: I didn't abandon myself, apologize, or make myself small.

Persistence: It wasn't going well, but I didn't give up.

Shamelessness: I didn't let myself feel embarrassed about the situation he created.

Boldness: I asked for what I wanted from those around me.

Honesty: I told the truth as it was happening.

And because those muscles had gotten strong from hours of stage time, I was able to withstand that experience without letting it consume me or take me out of the game. At my sister's request, I did stop going to that particular mic for a few weeks. She was worried for my safety and she had a good point. Embarrassed man-bears are known to seek revenge. But eventually I went back and learned that the man had left town. Apparently, he'd been getting into trouble at several local bars and took off.

You don't show up, but almost. I didn't know that was called tailgating, I thought that was fatherhood.

He quit the Town. But me? I hadn't quit comedy.

Since that early heckling experience, I've had dozens more like it and through these experiences and watching other comics manage them, I've learned how to defend that space. How to distract, change direction, shut it down quickly, and effectively move the attention back to where I want it.

The more time I spent on stage the more I began to realize that what I was learning on stage 100% applied to real life. The audience is the embodiment of the other, any person other than you, whether that's friend or foe. You want other people on your side. You want to feel connected, but you don't always. Maybe you start in a weird way or you say something that puts them off. Or maybe they just don't like you, for whatever reason. You want them to like you, but just like in regular life, sometimes wanting that too much is a turnoff. So, you learn to play it cool. *Be cool, man, just be cool.* I work too hard to get there to not learn how to do that. If you talk to most comics, they understand it's part of the job. We don't like it, we don't usually want you to heckle, but if we learn to deal with it effectively and even humorously then we become hecklerproof. We become the queen of our own stage.

The Taxes and Penalties on Attention

The problem with dealing with hecklers is that it does re-ignite some of that old hide-and-seek energy I talked about earlier. It's great to get on stage, speak up, and shine my light for all the world to see. But shining a light can attract predators.

I've had my experiences with predators well before I ever took the stage as a stand-up comic.

When I was 17, I attended a pagan gathering in the wooded hills of southern Indiana. At night, the folks of the camp would gather in a geodesic dome set into the side of a hill and play music, sing, and dance around a bonfire all night and into the dawn. As someone who had been taking dance classes from a young age, this scene captivated me. From the first day I arrived I spent every night dancing, entranced by the drums, the firelight, the chants. It was a highly formative time in my life when I was

CHAPTER X - ALL YOUR COURAGE

bridging my physical gifts of movement with my spiritual awareness—all in the company of a friendly and warm community. The gathering consisted of a closely-knit bunch of healers, musicians, and folks who engaged in alternative types of spirituality. What brought everyone together was the love of the land, of nature and of expanding awareness.

So, then you can imagine how open and relaxed I was feeling when one night as I took a break from circling the fire and was hanging out on the sidelines, an older man approached me. He was about 50 years old, tall, with glasses. He was dressed in hippy style clothing with some kind of handwoven poncho, sandals and a large brimmed hat with short brown hair creeping out from underneath. Something about him felt a little off, like he was in costume or didn't quite belong there. I'd seen him watching me dance around the fire, but then a lot of people were. I quickly shoved those feelings aside as he complimented my dancing and started engaging me in conversation. He told me he was a healer and I found this intriguing. I was just beginning to learn about the world of holistic healers and had spent a lot of time talking with different practitioners at this particular gathering. He explained that he knew a special method of using a light to look into people's pupils. He said by doing so, he'd be able to tell me if there was anything wrong with my internal organs. Apparently, my liver, intestines and other innards would reveal themselves underneath his special light. He asked me, "Would I like him to take a look at my eyes?"

I was intrigued, "For free?" He generously nodded. *Okay, well why not?* I thought.

The tall older costumed man convinced me he needed total darkness to do it though. In order to see everything properly, the light by the firelight would not do and *Would I go with him into a dark shack on the side of the dome where we could be alone?* Some part of me hesitated, but I brushed any concern away by thinking, *Ah this is a friendly community* and *everyone here is safe, right?*

He led me out of the dome and up the stairs to a little shack just outside. It looked like someone's backyard shed put together by one of those Home Depot kits only maybe 40 years ago. It was practically crumbling apart with decay. Inside it was pitch dark and so he used his special light to be able to see and rummaged around pulling out a couple of buckets for us to sit on. He started talking me through the process—telling me what he was going to do before he would do it just like I imagined a healer might. He held his special light up to my eyes—which just looked like an ordinary pin light you might have on the end of your keychain—and I winced uncomfortably against the bright light in my eye. His voice soothed me *just one moment, just one moment more* as he slowly moved the light from one eye to the other, a studious look on his face. Then he started to talk about healing. His voice low and gentle he talked about different energetic blockages we can carry in our bodies. "Sometimes you can carry emotions in your heart." He touched my chest lightly just above my breasts. "Sometimes you can carry the weight of something in your spleen." He tapped underneath my ribs. My body went very still with his touches. I was confused. He was a healer, right? This was okay? He was just touching my organs.

The light in my eyes was beginning to make me blind. I couldn't see his face, only felt his touch and the constant banter of his calm voice as he continued to tap me here and there. "And then there are other places that need healing. Sometimes we need sexual healing," and with those last words he moved his hand deftly up under my skirt and touched me in my groin. At this, some smarter part of me shook out of the trance and bolted out of there.

I jumped up and barged out of the shack and back towards the dome scurrying down the steps. My eyes had a hard time adjusting at first and I stumbled but I kept going. I couldn't move fast enough to get back to the other people and the music. It was just a moment, just a flash, just a touch, but I never forgot that experience: dancing and shining my light but then attracting the unwanted attention that came with it.

And these kinds of hide-and-seek experiences found me again and again.

Being 20 years old and trying to explain to a Saudi-Arabian audience member at the restaurant where I performed in Indianapolis why I wouldn't "lay" with him because a belly dancer in the United States is not a synonym for sex worker.

Being 22 and on a trip in Israel when I fell sick with a fever and my friend's roommate tried to rub some kind of vinegar solution over my chest and breasts to try and "help."

Being 25 and having my college philosophy professor tell me that if I wasn't pregnant, he would love to have his way with me to get back at his cheating wife.

Being 35 and having a male choreographer pull a piece from my showcase two days before the show because I wouldn't sleep with him.

Being 37 and having a very drunk audience member follow me backstage and try to force himself on me when I was alone in the dressing room.

Being 45 and having a showrunner no longer book me because I refused his advances....

And on and on. Experiences like these pile up in the corners of my mind. Remember earlier when I talked about taking things off the shelf? Well, there are some things you never want to take back out. You cast them just outside of the closet. Just outside of your memory's peripheral view where they collect dust in the lost-and-found box of your mind. You don't want to own them. You desert these awful souvenirs and hope they get taken by somebody else or tossed in the trash. But part of stepping into your queen years is about integrating these things that have happened: rummaging around in this lost-and-found box and loving yourself enough to let go of the pain and reclaim these abandoned parts of yourself.

Not only does sharing these #metoo memories here help me reintegrate them to myself, but I also share them as a way to hopefully underline the complexity of the currency of attention.

It's not a straightforward game of getting it or giving it.

The attention currency (especially in the world of those who identify as women) is a complex one that comes with taxes and unforeseen penalties.

That's why I've spent my whole life in a game of hide and seek with it. And maybe you have, too.

Because performing isn't just something we do on stage.

As we move from being young girls through puberty and into adulthood, we play a variety of roles and try on different characters. There are all kinds of ways that you and I perform in the face of hecklers and predators.

Erupting ferocious man-bears in bars, the business partner trying to take advantage of you, the person catcalling you on the street—I would like to tell you that one day you won't have these encounters. That I can teach you a way to avoid them. That I can protect you from the violence, harassment, and hurt of this world. Sadly, I can't. What I've come to learn is that, unfortunately, we live in a world full of sick and hurt people who will go on to infect and hurt others in contortions and that these experiences are a part of being human in a sick world.

For years, there has been an unconscious belief hiding deep inside me that because I kept attracting predatory behavior that something was wrong with me. I was doing it all wrong. Shining my light but too bright or in a weird way. There was something wrong inside of me that was making all of this happen to me. When the actual truth of my queen years has surfaced recently and I've learned that there is nothing wrong with me. These things just happen. I may encounter them again in my lifetime much to my chagrin. But I can lessen the impact, I can learn to use my "no" and remember that I always have a choice—this helps me navigate the emotions that instances like these leave in their wake.

For so many years I thought there was something in me that was attracting this behavior. The old, "What were you wearing?" but even deeper. For my entire life I've been made to feel bad or wrong for my sensuality. Flashback to the church boy who criticized me for doing the splits in a skirt. My entire life people have told me I'm acting sexy when sex isn't on my mind. Simply being an embodied person, a sensory person, a woman with curves, and a joyous friendly personality, a person who enjoys performing, and appreciating others with words that others take to be flirtatious has made me a target for criticism that I'm too sexy, too much. In my mind I am loving, and yet to others I am enticing. This has caused so much confusion, so many contortions, and made me feel like I was made wrong. It was so deeply embedded that I had forgotten that it was even there. But recently I've come to understand that I am *not* wrong. I am a loving, embodied person in a sick, stunted world full of contortions.

Does the pain ever go away? Will there ever be a point where I am done? Fully healed?

My Wise Woman answers, *"Not really. Things won't cease happening to you, but you will deal with them better with time."*

Can we board up our soul's windows, build walls, hide true selves in the basement in hopes that the creeps and sick people of the world won't be able to get to us?

No. Not without deeply affecting our availability to love and connection. Not without contorting ourselves into unrecognizable shapes.

So then where do we find our power in the face of hecklers and predators?

Remember the Tempestas.

The Tempestas Faces the Hecklers

It's great to be the Tempestas. To turn around the energy of everything you encounter, to change the temperature of the room, but the only way you become that is by learning the emotional fluency I was talking about earlier. And that means being okay with yourself even when you're not the Tempestas. It's a paradox. In the surrender to the outcome, you can sometimes control the outcome.

But the queen knows better than to bank her happiness on outcomes.

I am learning to find my strength in every moment. Even when I feel weak. In the honesty of that there is also strength. That's what we need to learn in order to be bold, to ask for what we want, to be provocatively honest, to be shameless, to stay in the game, and be loyal to ourselves. We don't have to get rid of our negative emotions. We just have to be able to learn to feel them without becoming them. We have to learn to regulate them and refocus ourselves so they don't rule us, we rule them.

Being able to navigate your own emotions is one thing, but also isn't it sweet to be able to stare down the bullies, put people in their place, and fend off the hecklers of the world? Emotional fluency is powerful, but to become the Tempestas it doesn't hurt to also know how to handle others.

Here's what often can happen to comics. We get mean. We may try to make a joke of it or pass it off or keep going, but if it goes on too long, we can become bitter. We have worked really hard on these jokes honing them over many many sets at shitty open mics at bars at crappy venues where we've had to sit around for hours trying to not become an alcoholic. When someone in the crowd starts trying to derail it, we are fucking pissed. Understandably so! I envy comics who have a mean or even just grumpy stage persona. If a heckler goes for them, it's absolutely in their character to shoot them down. And they stay true to their own game.

Beautiful.

But for most of us, getting really mad is an example of not being in control. This is falling prey to the fight-or-flight response and losing our emotional fluency. We have to learn how to be who we are without stooping to handle a situation that's chomping at the bit to bring us down. And there it is in a nutshell: the assumption that people are trying to bring us down.

The truth is that people want to be seen. They want to feel included or heard. They want to be the life of the party. They want their friends to think they're funny. Or… okay, maybe once in a while they just don't like you and they want to take you down! But they've known you for five seconds. How much can that really be about you? (It never is).

We have a few options.

The Tactic: Be flexible. Give them what they want. On your terms.

Throw them a bone. I do this when I believe it will be more fun to play with them and I'm at a place in my set where it makes sense. It feels fun to put attention on them and I know it won't suck me into a hole I can't get out of. I shine the spotlight on them and dominate them with questions. I am 100% in control even though I am shifting attention to them for a moment. This makes them the butt of the joke. You are making an example of them that can discourage other potential hecklers. The downside is that they might see it as an opportunity to make the night about them. You had better have a good, loud microphone, some distance between you and the person, and some bouncer backup to try this method.

The Tactic: Ignore them.

When there is an audience member who is so incredibly drunk or rowdy that I can feel it will just spiral out of control if I give them attention, sometimes I will literally turn my entire body away from that side of the audience. Instead of acknowledging them, I'll focus on the people in the crowd that are listening to what I'm saying in a very determined manner and completely ignore the interruptions. I'll give them no attention. No energy. I can feel if I feed them, they'll just keep going, but if I ignore them, they will give up. The important thing is to not allow myself to carry any emotional charge or attachment to the hecklers' attempts. I must stop the flow of energy towards them entirely.

The Tactic: Do something unexpected.

Another approach is to throw your plans to the wind and do something they don't expect. This was an approach that the singer, Jewel, learned to use when she was first starting out in her career:

> I got heckled a lot in bars. I had to learn how to be witty and quick on my feet. I figured out entertainer tricks to get people to listen. I would sometimes tell people, "I'd like to invite everyone here who doesn't want to see me to leave." I remember once when I was opening for Neil Young I couldn't get their attention so I just started whispering. I whispered and I got the whole audience to be quiet.

The Tactic: Give them attention, ignore them, then call in some help.

If nothing works, it's time to ask for help. A producer, club owner, security, another comic friend. Though, to be honest, I have had one person do this for me. Other times I have stood around looking towards producers who are talking to comics backstage rather than paying attention to me. And venues or show runners will not always step in right away. That's why comics get so good at dealing with it. There's simply no other way to finish your set without dealing with your heckler. It's like that campfire song, *Going on a Bear Hunt*:

> *Going on a bear hunt!*
>
> *Gonna catch a big one.*
>
> *I'm not afraid.*
>
> *But what's that up ahead?*
>
> *It's a giant mud puddle!*
>
> *Can't go over it.*
>
> *Can't go under it.*
>
> *Can't go around it.*
>
> *Gotta go through it.*

Sometimes it's not going to go well and you just have to get through it. Sometimes, if nothing else is working and I wait patiently in silence long enough, the heckler will eventually either peter out or the audience will help bring them under control. Either way, it is obvious that I have lost control of the room; but at the very least I have stayed in conversation with myself (emotional fluency) and I still have control over me.

Owning Your Hard-Earned Attention

At the end of the day, the struggle with a heckler is all about attention. As comics and the ones with the mic in our hands we are clearly receiving a bunch of it and sometimes an audience might think we're not worthy of it.

A woman once said, "I could do better," in the middle of my set.

Or maybe they just want to grab a little slice of attention for themselves. They want to step into our spotlight and feel the warmth of that attention, even if they end up getting smacked down for it.

But if you're a comedian, you have worked damned hard to earn that attention. You have spent hours at countless open mics just to get your turn to do 3–5 minutes. You have spent months doing this, and then years, trying out new jokes, failing, sometimes winning. Editing your work to what exact words get the laughs, connecting, networking with other comics who run shows, asking to be booked, waiting to be booked, finally! Getting on the shows that you want to be on and then one dude having a wonky day decides to speak up during your hard-won moment to shine.

Fuck that guy. The attention we receive is hard earned. Yours and mine. How many extra hours did you have to put in at work or at home to find yourself in a position where all ears and eyes are on you for a second? We put in extra work to achieve the same thing. So that's why we have to protect that attention, learn how to defend the circumference of our spotlight, and make it impenetrable to the hecklers.

Making Magic Out of Madness

As queens, we want to defeat the bully every time, but more importantly, we want to maintain a sense of agency over our own emotions. And at our very best, we take the weird, unexpected disruptions in life and play with them, making them into something even better than we could have made up by ourselves. When we pair the control of ourselves with letting go of control of others—and learn to play on that field—sometimes magic can creep in.

CHAPTER X · ALL YOUR COURAGE

Like the time I was the headliner at StorySlam Alameda. I started running a storytelling show in early 2024 and found myself thrust into this other comedy-adjacent world of storytelling. Because people already knew me as a professional comedian, before I even knew quite what I was doing with it, I began getting booked on professional storytelling gigs. There are all kinds of these. There's the Moth, a storytelling competition that's held nationwide and has a very popular podcast. And then there's other local shows where some combination of amateurs and professionals get up and tell stories. Sometimes even the audience is asked to "put their name in the hat" for a chance at storytelling. On this particular night I was the headliner, which meant I was the one person on the show who would be paid and expected to perform at the end of the night after all the other participants had told their stories.

I got there at the start of the show and settled in with a table of other storytellers I know, ready to listen and enjoy the show before my set. This particular storytelling show was held at a comedy club and I don't know if it was because it was there or just the vibe of the night but the audience seemed to be more of a wild comedy crowd than a normal, reverent storytelling audience. Not that storytelling audiences don't laugh and enjoy themselves—they do—but this audience was a little rowdier and responded to every sentence like a punchline. It was a boisterous evening.

Finally, they got through all of the volunteer storytellers and it was my turn to close out the night as the featured storyteller. I got nervous as the MC appeared to be reading my entire life's story as she introduced me. Was this audience going to think I was too full of myself? Were they going to be able to hold space for some of the more somber moments of my story?

When I finally took the stage, I made a joke about it. "I think she just read my entire bio! Wow, okay!" I praised all of the storytellers of the night and acknowledged the rowdy crowd, mentioning how much

I'd enjoyed hearing everyone. I even did a couple of light jokes about particular stories, lightly roasting the most recent storyteller who gave an account of a wild night of partying. "This guy here, have you even gone to bed since that story happened?" The crowd laughed. They understood that I was there to connect with them and would be entertaining. I was connected and able to start my story.

Lucky for me that night, I had picked a story that started with an audience participation element. "Raise your hand if you studied Spanish in middle school." They raised their hands, strengthening the connection. I could feel their participation bubbling up, serving up more. I allowed it, stopped feeding it too much, waited until it crested, and began to fall off before really launching into my story. I progressed carefully, making sure I stayed connected to the people listening, who were maybe a little drunk, but also willing to follow along with me.

I proceeded through my story that was already written, allowing it to live in the room, allowing their presence to shape how I delivered parts of it. Waiting for the laughter, allowing it to drive the way I said the next sentence and the next. Allowing their participation but not letting it pull me fully off course. And somehow, carefully, with conviction, I was able to pull them into the sad parts of the story with me. The part of the story that had real feelings and was hard to tell. I had to drop any affectation. Any need for it to go a certain way. I had to let myself feel into those feelings and let the room hold them for me. This wasn't acting. This was a recounting of my own true story.

I really and truly allowed this story to become what it was supposed to be with that particular crowd on that particular evening. There were funny bits where there weren't before. I was present to people's reactions, to the waves and ebbs and flows of emotion. I stayed grounded and when I said the last few lines of that story, it felt like I was pulling a really expensive car into the garage after leading a parade. We had gone on an adventure together,

CHAPTER X · ALL YOUR COURAGE

but now I was bringing them all home with me and it felt satisfying and safe.

Later I reflected on the night and recognized how much skill it took to do all of that. It is so easy to get thrown off the path by other people's reactions. How many times do people take what you say wrong? Or aren't as interested in what you have to say as you think you warrant? Everyone wanted to participate and be a part of it. I could have led as a dictator and no one would have had fun. Instead, I allowed them to take part in it, to say to them, "Yes, you are here. You matter. You are helping me do this." Every particle of my being was grateful for them every step of the way, even as things didn't go as I thought they would.

I used my honesty. I stayed loyal to myself. I was shameless and persistent even in moments when I stumbled. I kept asking for what I wanted (their attention) and stood in my worthiness to get it. Those who were potential hecklers unknowingly became my collaborators because I refused to let their interactions be felt as detractors, but rather incorporated them as a part of the experience. I didn't get defensive. I didn't just flee or abandon myself up there, and I kept the energy moving and didn't let anything freeze. And through these skills I was able to be a vessel of charisma transmitting courage.

I was pretty proud afterwards as I reflected on how many hours of taking it on the chin with hecklers, bullies, and harassers interrupting or worse it took for me to be able to navigate that. How many hours of playing in the sandbox it took for me to be able to do that so deftly that it didn't even appear to be a skill. The maneuvering was so good that it was invisible.

And that is the skill I want for every queen.

Let's face it. The world doesn't want us to have power, so in some ways it isn't the worst thing when it's so good they don't see it coming.

You've done a lot of the training already. I don't know a single queen who hasn't been through their lion's share of hecklers, harassers, and predators in everyday life. You've met those man-bears in the woods.

So, now is the time to trust that training, be present, and go.

Leading up to now, this book has been about honing the courage you need to face down life's hecklers and get their attention, but the rest of this is about what you do when you capture it. You've played the fool; you've won some battles. Truly stepping into your queen years is about transcending all of that and returning you and your people to health. It's about using a skill you may or may not have realized you've been honing all along.

Get ready because this next part is going to satisfy your twelve-year-old Ouija board-at-slumber-parties self. It's going to blow away her satisfying girl scout cookie sales and might even trump the experience of her first French kiss.

Because this next part isn't just about pleasure; it's about power, too.

Your power, you freaky little psychic witch.

Yes, you.

Let's talk about these gifts you've been hiding....

CHAPTER XI

That's My Time: Shining a Light on Others

I'm psychic. I can see things before they happen. The other night I ate half of a sheet cake and threw the rest away, but I knew I was going to go back and eat the rest of that sheet cake out of the garbage later that night. Psychic!

I have a psychic bit that I do onstage when I'm performing comedy that I call, *Reading your relationship auras... against your will.* Maybe you've seen me do it? I probably learned a bit of this from my dad. He always prided himself on being psychic and had an uncanny knack for finding things that were lost or knowing things he shouldn't. It was a terrible thing to have a psychic dad as a teenager! He knew when I snuck off with boys, wasn't telling the truth, or was hiding something I did. But I do think I inherited a bit of my intuition from him.

Anyhow, this psychic bit that I do developed organically one night when I was performing at one of my regular venues in Oakland. My usual material wasn't working. It was landing flat and, honestly, I wasn't having fun doing it. So not knowing what else to do, I started talking to people. A lot of comics, when they do crowd work, begin by asking people in the audience questions, but I did the opposite. I pretended to be psychic and started *telling* people about themselves.

It started with a good-looking couple in the front row. He had her arm around her but in a polite way and her delicate hands were resting in her lap. They both were dark-haired, dressed for the night out but in neutral colors and still a little business casual, like they were auditors and couldn't be bothered with flash. They had been laughing a bit but in a restrained way like they were a little scandalized by everything I said. Perfect subjects to mess with. The words came out of my mouth without barely thinking, "Oh you two, you've been together, what? Two years? And you met at a school?" They nodded their heads in surprise!

"And you," I pointed to the woman. "You are still in school right now, grad school maybe, and it is putting a little strain on things because he is having to do more of the shopping, the cooking, the cleaning, am I right?" They looked stunned. He vigorously nodded, so I continued playfully, "It's payback time, buddy! Suck it up and get used to it! And move your big-ass shoes out of the doorways!" In that moment, the air of surprise into the room turned into a bloom of laughter and I moved on to the couple behind them.

"All right, there's a lot of chemistry here. It's hot. I'm thinking it's been about four months, am I right?" The couple nodded. They couldn't be sitting any closer together and they have that new love energy, so that was an easy guess, but then something else floats to my mind, "I'm getting the sense that you don't like her mother?" The man made a face that was sadly rueful. "Well, guess what… she doesn't like you either!" And the fun continued.

CHAPTER XI - THAT'S MY TIME

The first time I did this it was a strange rapid fire. I didn't stop to think about what I was doing. I just opened my mouth and said the first things that came to mind as I looked at people in the audience. Each time getting more specific in my claims and each couple confirming my psychic readings were correct.

It was Saturday, date night, so there were endless couples in the room. "You two!" I zeroed in on a couple of women who were sitting in a pair of chairs tucked around a cocktail table. One glance at their cocktails and their proximity and I could tell they are probably best friends. "You two have been friends forever, but there's definitely been some kind of making out in the bathroom of a bar once when you were drunk." They switched from shock to laughter right away. They glanced a little nervously at each other as I said, "Yep, there's definitely a bit of romance, maybe even since middle-school but then it was a little weird and you decided *I'm not all that gay and hmm let's just go buy Sketchers and flirt with boys at the mall.*" The laughter in the room was rolling, meaning I barely got out the sentence before the sound reached up and drowned out the end.

I turned to a table squarely to my right. "And you!" The room suddenly fell silent. Everyone wanted to hear what I had to say. I relished how commanding this bit was. The tension was high because everyone was afraid I might come at *them*. It was so delicious I couldn't help myself. Before saying anything else, I turned to look at the audience and give a mischievous smile. It coaxed an excited laugh out of the crowd. I turned back to the couple. They were an interesting pairing. She had the kind of high-maintenance beauty that reminds me of Instagram models; all eyelashes, great makeup contouring, breasts popping out of her top just perfectly, and he's the complete opposite—just real down-to-earth normal-looking dude with glasses. I quickly clocked that one of his shoes was untied and his hair was disheveled and not in an intentional way. "Y'all are an interesting pair. You have a lot in common, like you both like pizza and dog videos." The couple nodded while the audience laughed at the banality of my guess. I moved on, "And you really like this guy for his kindness and intellect." Our Instagram model nodded enthusiastically in agreement. "Yeah, I can *see* that," I said, emphasizing the word *see*. I repeated it for comic effect, "I can *see* that."

Then something caught my attention and I looked to the back of the room at a large bachelorette party; they were all wearing matching pink tops with cheesy legends like, "I make pour decisions" and "Hakuna moscato" and the bride was wearing a white headband with a comically tiny netted veil. "And you!" I turned my attention to them so quickly, I startled the bride, who jolted and spilled white wine on her top. "Your husband-to-be's name is Brad!"

"Oh my gawd!" one of the bridesmaids exclaimed loudly as the bride's jaw dropped. This claim hung in the air as everyone waited in suspense to find out if this could be right. The bride regained control of her jaw, gulped, and said, "Brett."

"Whoa!" I said as I think *this is so weird... How am I doing this right now?* I confirmed with the bride, "I don't know you, right? We did not talk before the show, correct?" The bride nodded "Well, y'all, what can I say? I'm psychic." I could see the audience trade glances, mouth, "wow," and, "oh my god!" at each other, and break into applause.

The trance was over then, but it had been a funny, organic bit that came about because I had nothing else to say while being really tuned in and connected to the audience. Eventually, as I played with this bit more and more on stage, I would tell the audience, "I'm going to read your relationship aura against your will." People found that idea really funny and a little intimidating (*what if she really can?*), so it became a thing.

At the time all this started developing I was producing my show, The Comedy Edge on the Waterfront, performing to a crowd of 150–200 people a week, many of them returning regulars. As a comic, it's difficult to come

CHAPTER XI · THAT'S MY TIME

up with all new material every week unless you love bombing the entire time so I decided to use the relationship-aura bit in the middle of every set to keep it fresh for the regulars and myself. The nice thing about it is that I get to exercise my intuition. I make these psychic attempts, but the nice thing is that if I'm wrong, I just make silly comments to make it funny. I can make it work either way. Either I'm correct and getting immediate feedback on my psychic skills or I'm wrong and it's all a joke anyway.

The question I get asked most by people after I do this bit at a show is, "Are you really a psychic?"

My answer is always, "Yes, I am psychic and so are you."

I really do believe that we all have this gift of intuition. It's a byproduct of empathy. When we open ourselves to feeling other people's feelings and pay attention to them, we can see things we might have missed before. Or we get hits on what might be going on for them. We all have the power to tap into that gut instinct and feel things in other people. It's just a matter of whether or not we choose to develop that.

This kind of powerful empathy appears in cultural traditions around the world. Documented instances of supposed extrasensory ability date as far back as ancient Greece, particularly the Oracle of Delphi. And as women stepping into our queen years, we are at a time in our lives when we are primed to work on this kind of thing based on our physiology alone. There has been little research but lots of speculation that the hormonal shifts, particularly drops in estrogen, that come with menopause lead to changes in the temporal lobe in the brain, an area associated with, one of many things, your intuition.

A lot of people identify as empathetic and will describe it as something they have to deal with—a burden to bear. What if it isn't a burden but a superpower?

Sensitivities Become Superpowers

Most of us are familiar with the psychological profile of the empath. I identify as an empath—don't even ask me to go see a horror movie! It will live inside me and haunt me forever! So I would imagine that many of my fans and friends also might identify as being empathic. An empath is highly attuned to the energy and emotions of those around them. They can have a hard time in crowds, watching scary movies, or hearing someone's story about how they got injured. Empaths are known for taking on the emotions of others as their own.

The problem with being an empath is that when you sense the emotions of other people it can feel disorienting, confusing, and you feel tossed about emotionally based on the emotional atmosphere of what's going on around you. It can be immensely overwhelming. But on the other side of that emotional super-sensitivity, there are also powerful skills to be used. As we gain emotional fluency, our sensitivities become superpowers. Empathic tendencies are no longer a hindrance. They are gifts that come in packages labeled "Handle with care." We may require a higher level of delicate handling, but we're figuring out what that looks like and there are benefits that come along with it. We've got access to a whole other level of knowledge coming from the world around us, sometimes even opening the door to psychic awareness and more advanced intuition.

In my journey with stand-up comedy, as I've been learning how to connect and be present with an audience, I've experienced an interesting side effect. The attention on myself has started to take a back seat in importance to the power of attention that I have to give others. I actually find myself becoming more empathic and more psychic, which has made me realize there is another level to being an empath. When you can learn how to stay with yourself, while also feeling what someone else is feeling, you can become a more powerful empath. Instead of potentially collapsing under the weight of other people's feelings, I've learned to be able to feel, listen, and play with the present without allowing it to dictate my reaction or my mood.

When empaths become queens, so long as we continue the journey of self-knowledge and exploration, we have the potential to become more aware of our psychological edges. And when we do that, we can harness our psychic inclinations and channel them into becoming an Empathic queen.

The Profile of the Empathic Queen

The Empathic Queen can easily distinguish between their own emotions and someone else's.

The Empathic Queen is able to shift their attention elsewhere before they become too overwhelmed with feeling someone else's feelings.

The Empathic Queen develops tools to help them receive these messages from other people without taking them on as their own. They learn the delicate balance of staying empathetic while also staying in a zone that is still helpful.

The Empathic Queen regularly practices their mind-body connection whether it's through meditation, hypnosis, or somatic practices such as mindfulness, yoga, dance therapy, etc.

The Empathic Queen stays curious and open towards others and is okay with being wrong about something. They welcome the dialogue and are more interested in the truth than they are in being correct.

The Empathic Queen is responsible with their observations. They learn to trust their instincts, but know better than to draw assumptions. Even when they're receiving something, they are still filtering it through their own worldview, their own beliefs and agenda. It is always more responsible to ask questions and allow others to come into their own awareness of what an empath is sensing rather than forcing an idea on them.

The Empathic Queen knows the power of laughter. They can fill a room with lightness, pop the tension with humor and go into the heart of what's really happening without losing sight of the universal joke of it all.

The Empathic Queen is committed to the regular practice of emotional fluency.

The Empathic Queen is committed to their own emotional health and stability so as not to be vulnerable to taking on too much energy from other people.

The Empathic Queen practices self-loyalty, honesty, shamelessness, boldness and persistence.

Moving Attention Inwards and Outwards

The best way to begin honing your ability as an Empathic Queen is by learning how to distinguish yourself from the outside world by separating what is yours and what is not yours; what is true to you and your being and what is something you're picking up. Knowing the difference between those two things is crucial. Here's why. If you don't know where you end and where the rest of the world begins then how are you going to to tell the difference between what you are receiving externally and what you are getting from the fucked-up, traumatized, or critical voices in your head? How will you avoid projecting your reality onto other people? If you aren't able to separate your ego, and see your judgments clearly, you won't be able to receive helpful, intuitive messages.

When I was a little kid through my early adulthood, I was painfully empathetic. I've always picked up on things, like other people's feelings and the atmosphere of my surroundings. When you're a child you don't know any better; you take it on and make it yours. You're right there in it, so how do you recognize it? You don't know what's yours and what's not. And in one form or another, I took that on. Not only did I take on the emotions of other people, I would play into the expectations of what other people thought of me. I was so sensitive to what they felt and thought that I would pick up a story and pour myself into the role they had written for me. Then together we would play out a weird melodrama. Other people's expectations were so powerful over me it felt like I had no choice but to go along with them. When I was around someone that assumed I was a ditz, I became a bubbly ditz. When I was around someone that expected me to be apologetic, I would fall all over myself apologizing. It worked great as an actor. I would pour myself easily into a role and other people's expectations, but it was hell on my sense of self.

When I became a mother, the empathy took on a new tenor. When my kid experienced a hurt, I experienced a hurt. When he went through puberty, I felt like I was going through my own kind of second puberty. My son emphatically forbids me from telling his stories, so I won't give examples, but suffice to say that motherhood for me was an extreme training in empathy. I was thrust into a deep bond tying me to this vulnerable human and at the same time another part of me felt like it was straining for independence and fighting to keep myself and dreams alive. In many ways it was the beginning of my queen years training. These days

I can still feel the pull of other people's expectations, but I'm so aware of it that I don't allow myself to play into it anymore.

So, if you are an empath, then the first step to using it as a superpower is to start being able to separate out: This is mine. That's yours. I don't need to own it. I don't need to hold it. I don't even need to pay attention to it. As long as it's not dangerous to me, I'm not even looking over there. By being able to separate ourselves from others, we begin to build the self so that it is so strong that other people's energies don't just flow in and sway us, pull us off of our centers, or make us a puppet of their expectations.

So, how do I begin to do this?

The key is to become dexterous when focusing our attention both inwards and outwards.

When I was a student at Tamalpa Institute learning the Art/Life process, a lot of time was spent on somatic exercises, where we got in touch and expressed how our body felt, what our emotions were, what we imagined, etc. Only once you put your finger on your own experience, were you invited to express what you "imagined" and "saw or heard" of someone else's experience. Through this exercise I became so much clearer about what parts of what I was feeling were my own feelings. My own story, my own assumptions, my own emotions.

When I was able to feel something and identify it as mine, I became keenly aware of what was foreign. That became my doorway to my psychic ability. And when I also learned to shift my attention away so it wouldn't attach itself to me or gain energetic momentum, then the Empathic Queen began to emerge.

Practicing Your Attention Inwards

So, what does the regular practice of focusing inwards look like? It can be any kind of introspective practice, meditation, hypnosis, yoga, breathwork, bodywork, somatic practices, or mindfulness moving practice of any kind. It can be going outside and talking to the trees...the ways you can do this are as varied as there are humans. I know for so many of us we balk at creating a regular practice that focuses inward because we can come across uncomfortable feelings and it's tough to face those; and it's also difficult to focus ourselves on the task at hand. Our attention is slippery and needs training.

Any time I lie down to start doing meditation my thoughts go something like this:

> *Wow, I'm really actually very good at this. Look at me relaxing. Not thinking of anything. It's like that time when I used to meditate every day and I could just take a nap whenever. Look at me not thinking of...oh right whoops heh heh okay... uhhh BREATHE... Look at me not thinking of any— BREATHE. Look at argggh, okay, focus on the good relaxed feeling and take it downnnnn... ahhhh...I'm feeling pretty relaxed in my back. Okay, yeah. That feels nice, but my hip has been bothering me lately even though it isn't right now...feels kind of dead near there actually—no: dead. That's a bad word, don't think that... Oh, don't think. Just relax, yes, BREATHE.*

You see? Very slippery! My attention is like a wandering child! If I stick with it, though, slowly but surely, I do find a way to focus on those naturally good feelings in my body. Then, truth be told, I will often fall asleep at this point. Probably because I don't get enough sleep at night, or because I'm a real snorer (an ex-boyfriend called my snoring *aggressive!*). But about half the time I am able to fully relax and still hover my awareness above sleep or unconsciousness. I'll often focus on my body and the sensations that I start to feel when I really allow myself to drop down and feel them. I am someone who experiences acute interoception, my brain's representation of sensations from my own body. I can sense my heart beating and the pulsing of blood, but I can feel things even beyond that. I feel flutters and waves of energy over my face. It's almost like I can feel the vibration of my molecules. It's the coolest thing to experience. So much so that I can almost visually see it in my mind's eye as it happens. It reminds me of one of those screensavers that are just waves of color that streak across the screen.

I can feel what I like to think of as my *energetic body*—the part of me that is non-physical or perhaps simply more electrical—moving, hovering, and never stopping. As I scan around my body I can sense different waves in different parts of my body. Sometimes they go from my legs up to my head or vice versa. Sometimes I sense heat in different areas. By allowing my mind to relax away from the everyday chatter of my thoughts, I am able to put my attention squarely on my energy body.

When I'm able to do this then I begin imagining that I'm moving things around—almost as though I'm rearranging the furniture in my mind. I'm releasing negative charges, emotions as they arise, seeing where my body is storing them, trying to breathe light into areas that are hurting and overall tune everything right up. Maybe I am even able to put a few old memories away into boxes in the closet of my mind. When I'm complete, I open my eyes and I feel refreshed. After doing this kind of meditation intuitive abilities are at an all-time high. Once I am so deeply tuned into myself, everything else feels bigger and louder and a different vibration by comparison.

It feels like it just got sharpened like a knife and I have a more conscious ability to point my attention wherever I want it to go. Our lives are so full of things that vie and battle for our attention, like social media, our phones, the lure of my couch, and Netflix, that I can just lose touch with my own agency over my choices. What is it that I want to do with myself right now? Where do I actually want to put my attention? Meditation places the sculpting knife of attention squarely back into my hands. So, if you want to become an Empathic Queen then it's important to find some practice like this for yourself.

CHAPTER XI - THAT'S MY TIME

Why bother? An empath is only as powerful as the focus of their attention. Psychic gifts, such as channeling, astral travel, and being empathic can cause suffering when we do not do the work of owning our stories, healing the hurt, and becoming emotionally fluent. We often don't want to do it or say we can't do it because it's painful or simply difficult, our attention wanders. But detaching from the wandering is part of the process. It's a bit like going to the gym. When you first start, if you haven't been working out much, you may need to reactivate entire muscle groups that you weren't using. But you don't just throw your hands up and quit. No, you take it easy at first, developing those muscles slowly and building trust with your body. The same is possible with your mind.

Illumination

If judging, manipulating, or dominating people is the contortion of outward attention, then what is the opposite? What is the higher purpose of attention itself? As Empathic Queens, what is possible when we focus our attention on other people?

In 2004, I took a trip through Rajasthan, in India—a state well-known for its majestic desert and royal cities. I was traveling with a group of dancers to research and learn the dances of the desert Romani people, known as the Kalbeliya. We had a driver, as a bunch of White ladies visiting India might do, who carted us from one town to the next and through the desert. His name was Amir and he regarded himself as a very good driver which we were about to find out was really quite relative. We had only barely gotten ourselves and our luggage tucked away inside the utility vehicle, and were still stuffing away our wallets into our hidden travel pouches, when Amir pulled out into the dusty freeway like the car itself was possessed. Swerving around other vehicles, people and buses loaded with people and all sorts of animals, he exhibited a calm ease at the wheel of his demon vehicle and eventually we settled in and accepted his manic driving.

What really impressed me about India was all the people everywhere. Rarely was there a space, either in the desert or in the cities, that was not full of people. I guess I'd heard it before, but it took seeing it to really get it. India was dense with humans. And as we were driving through a particularly dense town, Amir was forced to slow down to barely a crawl and it was then that I spotted a *Sadhu*, one of India's Hindu Holy Men. He was perched on some kind of divide in what appeared to be none other than the middle of traffic. He wore his hair in long locs, had tinted his skin white, and wore the smeared ash on his forehead that was customary of the Sadhu. He wore nothing other than a loincloth. His face was etched with a deep, contemplative frown. As we were completely stopped at that point, jammed in heavy traffic, I had plenty of time to take him in. He was not even a few feet away from me. Suddenly, feeling my stare, his eyes locked to mine and while maintaining his deep frown, he scowled. His face appeared hard and made of stone with two piercing eyes glaring out at me. It hit me in my soul.

At that moment I felt like an outsider. I thought he must hate me, this gawking tourist. My face felt hot and I felt the urge to look away in shame or embarrassment, but some little playful part of me decided to do something else. I held his gaze and I lifted my eyebrows in surprise. As he registered my face, something lightened a little, the stone face began to soften and shift. It was almost like watching some part of himself return. This made me smile. Then his face, too, blossomed into a genuine smile, revealing a chipped front tooth. It was endearing as hell and made me giggle a little. I felt relief wash over me from the top of my head down into my gut. The separation melted. Suddenly, we were connected across all vast cultural differences and we were just two people smiling goofily at one another separated only by a few feet and a glass window. We held

CHAPTER XI - THAT'S MY TIME

this gaze for a few seconds nodding and chuckling. Finally, the traffic eased up and our car lurched forward, onward towards our destination away from the smiling holy man.

What I experienced is something that author David Brooks might call *illumination*. He talks about this in his book *How to Know a Person: The Art of Seeing Others Deeply and Being Deeply Seen*. Illumination, as Brooks describes it, is projecting a quality of attention on a person that can bring out a different aspect of them. It can be a very powerful thing that we can give to others. In that moment with the Sadhu, by smiling I was reaching out to his playful side, the lightness in him that easily connects with anyone. Or, depending on how you read the story, it could have well been that he was calling forth the playfulness in me. It stands to reason that one can't fully know. I mean after all, *he* was the one who was praying.

"Attention," the psychiatrist Ian McGilchrist writes, "is a moral act: it creates, brings aspects of things into being."

You've probably experienced this loads of times. The grumpy store clerk perks up and glows when you point out her cute outfit, or conversely, when your sister brings up an old argument, you become guarded and feel like you have been time-warped to childhood. Our attention can bring out different aspects of a person. With our attention, we can not only shape the story of our own lives, but to some degree we can uplift the world of other people's as well.

So now as you are (hopefully) finally accepting the fact that the years of foolish games of grabbing for attention, or waging wars with attention are finally behind you, I can hear you wondering, "So, what am I supposed to do now? Just illuminate others? Just give my attention away? And that's it?"

CHAPTER XII

Attention: Wearing the Crown

Attention is bigger than we think and travels farther than we realize. Attention has the ability to dive to the cellular, mitochondrial depths of our bodies as well as shoot outwards into the far reaches of the universe and change dimension and form. From dreaming to studying to mindlessly scrolling or vegging out in front of the television to witnessing our tears, laughter, and terror, our attention has the capacity to travel everywhere we can imagine and carve out places we haven't imagined yet. Attention gets first dibs on tasting our own life's experiences and when we allow ourselves to feel empathy, it can also taste another's. We are never free of it and we never run out of it, but where it is directed matters more than anything. Where we decide to direct it can make all the difference in the lives that we lead.

One thing is for sure, attention is perhaps one of the most underappreciated gifts we have.

It's wild to think how much of our lives we spend squandering it. Worrying about getting it from others, fighting for attention with our siblings, our lovers, our friends, not to mention using our attention to look at screens and numb out on social media, losing hours of our life to mindless endless chatter while big brands and political forces manipulate our attention for domination, control, information, and profit. Then consider all of the things we do to try to grab attention or divert unwanted attention, all of these are games that commodify attention. Assume it to be a limited resource. When we play these games then our lives become a neverending performance.

The Never-Ending Performance

The popular coach, Mel Robbins, recently interviewed Dr. Zach Bush, MD, a board-certified physician specializing in hospice care. This man who spent so many hours with people who were dying reported on the similarity of people's words on their deathbed.

> The number one regret is, I was performing the whole time. I never was actually being me. And I was afraid to be me. I didn't even know what it would feel like to be me. But right now as I'm dying, as that veil thins and I feel myself and I'm a beautiful being and I am home. Wow, if I had just known I was whole the whole time and hadn't had to do all the performance...

Playing the Nice Girl, contorting ourselves to please others; these are all a performance and I'm well versed in it, as you know by now. I know you might be rolling your eyes to hear a performer suggest we all stop performing in life... but isn't it a little apt to hear it from someone who has felt the need and the compulsion to perform every aspect of their life? After all, I am still learning, too, even as I write this very book, how to give up my need for earning attention, for earning love and affection, and just learn how to accept it. How to receive it. How to let that shit in!

In my quest to step into my queen years powerfully, I've uncovered a secret. Attention is not the pawn in the game. Attention is the one

CHAPTER XII · ATTENTION: WEARING THE CROWN

playing the game... or choosing to quit the game and go do something else. Consciousness flows freely. It doesn't require a winner and a loser. It isn't a zero-sum game. Instead of being the object of attention I have become an enactor of it, wielding it powerfully to create a life that I want.

We are built to turn our consciousness in towards ourselves and outwards to others, alternating between the two. We are meant to pay attention to ourselves and also to other people in ways that create joy for ourselves as well as illuminate the best in others. Unfortunately, these outward and inward modes of attention have their own contortions. Instead of focusing on how we feel, our own emotions, the messages our bodies want to give us, we instead feel self-conscious. We feel the initial sting of an emotion and immediately add a story that we are bad, ugly, not smart, not worthy. We make assumptions about how other people feel about us. Our attention on ourselves is actually still attention on other people, or at least how we imagine other people think about us.

Life becomes a performance of how we think other people want us to be. We worry over these things beyond our knowing and beyond our control and allow them to shape our own beliefs, our own actions, and ultimately our lives. There's nothing wrong with having friends who support us and see the best in us, but we take this one step further and not only require it, but hinge our own selfworth upon it. We have forgotten the art of supporting ourselves from the inside.

> The deep dysfunction of relationships that we have on the planet right now is that we are trying to find somebody else that will make us feel good about ourselves. And more than that we are looking to another person to help us feel complete. And so we have this language, this is my better half, this is my partner, and you're going to cling onto that thinking you're gonna become complete. And you're going

to go into these many relationships to try and create this sensation of fullness or wholeness.

—Dr. Zach Bush, MD

We want to be seen so badly we disfigure and contort ourselves to get attention from our relationships. It's all a performance. We spend so much time worrying about where other people are putting their attention instead of being present to our own. But our own precious attention is where the power is. The real true majesty of attention is that we can create and move worlds by just focusing on our own.

When We Give Up the Game

As Tony Robbins said, "Where attention goes, energy flows." Through my own focus I've been able to change my story, create momentum in the areas of life I'm working on, and create an entirely new life for myself simply by trying and sometimes succeeding in harnessing this one simple thing.

Early in life we are scrambling for scraps of attention. We see attention as something to vie for, something to be coveted. We flirt with the power of it and then slowly it becomes a weapon. Ours and others. We wrestle around in the mud of manipulation and domination. But then something happens in our queen years. We become less concerned with any of that. Those games; yeah, we know them. We can play them when we have to but the value of attention becomes crystal clear.

The mud eventually settles to the bottom and we see that attention is about the power of creativity. Everything in our bodies is demanding that we revisit all of our old ways of working: the way we eat, the way we exercise, not to mention the past regrets and stories waiting to be addressed. It's all there asking for a glow up. Perimenopause invites us to become our own re-makers, like stylists of the soul. It is time to fashion ourselves and be the one to look in the mirror and say to ourselves, "I'm proud of you."

In a sense, we become our own mothers and have the opportunity to rebirth ourselves into the second half of our lives. And what else is rebirthing but learning how to create with our attention? Where our attention goes our stories grow. As a queen, you begin to recognize your attention as a gift, something with which to cultivate your own creativity and bestow upon others.

Creating with attention is getting out ahead of the need to go to war. It is using your attention to manifest and to play the game your own way.

Playing Your Own Game

Comedy is going great these days. I'm doing bigger shows and getting more opportunities, and also letting go of those times where I'm not the favorite. I'm learning to play the game the way it works for me.

As I neared my sixth year of comedy, I got to be a part of the San Francisco Comedy Competition. There are a ton of comedy competitions and I don't really care much about most of them but this one in particular has had some famous comedians like Robin Williams and Ellen DeGeneres compete in it. It is kind of a big deal and the only one I have ever been interested in doing. It's a pretty competitive process to even get in as only 32 comedians are accepted. The competition consists of multiple rounds and if you keep advancing it consumes a month of your life. After 20 shows they crown the winner.

When I got accepted as one of the 32, I was elated, but also nervous. With my recent hormonal changes, I had not been having what one might call a very winning year. Grief, depression, and anxiety plagued my day-to-day, and yet here was this opportunity. My therapist didn't even want me to do it. "Why put yourself in a position to be judged and in the line of fire when you aren't feeling emotionally strong?" But I didn't want to drop out. I'd always wanted to do the SFCC and here was my shot.

I decided my goal for this competition would not necessarily be to win against the other competitors per se, but to win at staying in solidarity with myself. Could I go through the shows while staying loyal to myself? Could I maintain my equilibrium and my integrity? Could I do my best and have fun while not worrying about winning? The judges were different every night and consisted of other comedians and random people in creative fields. Whether I won or not was really out of my hands. I wasn't going to be able to write an entirely new slamming set of hilarious material in the six weeks I had leading up to the competition. I might add some tags or maybe one new bit, but I had to go with what I already had, more or less. And the only thing I could control was my own mood and my vibration, how I felt.

I was determined to be at my highest vibration so here's what I did.

I meditated every single day. I cut back on drinking. I did all the healthy habits that have always helped me feel grounded at my best, like early morning walks, drinking enough water, cutting back on caffeine, sugar, alcohol. Eating my veggies. And most importantly, trying to feel as good as I could. Reminding myself to speak kindly towards myself. I made feeling good about myself my job. My most important job.

I also worked on my comedy. In the sets and shows I had leading up to the competition, I would evaluate my sets and notice things I could tweak, what I did well, and what needed improvement, but instead of judging myself, I practiced discernment. There was no, *that was bad, that was good,* but rather the feedback I gave to myself was *this worked and this didn't work.*

I practiced loyalty. On stage and in life I continued practicing boldness, shamelessness, honesty, and persistence. Anytime I ate it on

CHAPTER XII · ATTENTION: WEARING THE CROWN

stage I made a point of reveling in it, enjoying it even, dissecting where it turned and considering what I could have done differently.

I kept playing. I kept tweaking. But mostly I tried to have the most fun possible and be as light as possible about the outcomes. I was practicing, but more than getting the material right I was practicing the vibe, how I wanted to feel when I went through the competition.

Finally, the weekend of the competition came. The first night did not go as well as I had hoped. I was the 15th comic to perform. By the time I went up the audience had been listening for over an hour and a half and they were tired. I was tired. I went for it. Got laughs but a mild response in comparison to the other comedians. I felt disappointed. I felt annoyed by the other comedians who were jubilant and who were saying things like, "That was fun!" *Oh, was it? Did you have fun? Good for you*, I thought to myself bitterly. Luckily, I had the chance to vent to my friend, Jon Lehre who was also in the competition. He was encouraging and helped remind me that I vowed to have fun at this event.

The next morning, we had received an email from the producer letting us know who the top five comics were from the night before. I was not on that list. I was not surprised. He also mentioned that our scores would be "posted" that night so we could see where we fell in the ranking. I asked him what *posted* meant.

"Oh, it means that your total average score among all three judges will be shared."

"How will it be shared? I asked.

"On a piece of paper in the dressing room."

Got it. I vowed *not* to look at that piece of paper.

The next night we had two shows at the Guild Theatre in Menlo Park. It's an adorable mid-size theatre with a thrust stage and a lavish green room featuring several decadent rooms decorated with baroque touches of gold and bold patterns, wrap-around couches, and its own kitchen.

Hanging out in that green room made you feel like a rock star. Something clicked during that first set of the night amidst the posh accoutrements where my hunger to win kicked in. So, I gave it my all, tuned into the audience, and went for it. I had a great set.

On the second show of the night, we had some drunk heckler types. All the comics watched the show on the television monitor in our rockstar green room and we could see them pumping their fists in the air and getting up from their seats for drink refills. Comic after comic came offstage bemoaning these rowdy people who were interrupting their sets: Apparently it was a weird vibe out there because the front row cheered and laughed wildly while the rows of audience behind them were practically silent... with embarrassment? Possibly. Sometimes the audience gets turned off by audience members acting inappropriately and can clam up out of some kind of psychological need to distance themselves from the behavior. Either way, everyone was saying tonight was a nightmare; but something in me saw this as an opportunity to potentially pop the room.

Bring it on, I thought.

I had a game plan: I knew these unruly folks would interrupt me and I chose to not care. I decided I was going to love them. I knew I could handle it because for weeks I had been practicing feeling good no matter what. Something about being mid-way through the competition and not placing in the top five helped me recommit to my values and freed me up to not care quite as much. I was here to feel good. Here was my opportunity to really be tested. Could I enjoy myself no matter what they threw at me?

From the moment I walked out on stage they cheered wildly as they had been for all of the comics and I let it wash over me. In my mind, I pretended I was Freddie Mercury and this greeting was normal. I let it energize me. Instead of launching into my regular first joke I took a

CHAPTER XII · ATTENTION: WEARING THE CROWN

moment to acknowledge the strange crowd. "Okay! Well, you're a lively crew! I feel like this part of the audience," I pointed towards the drunken hecklers in front, "are acting like they're at a strip club... and this section," I gestured towards the quieter mild-mannered patrons behind, "are at church." The entire audience, front rows and back, let out a laugh of relief. Finally, I had acknowledged the elephant in the room. "I don't know if I have any jokes for either one of those places," I continued, "but we're about to *FIND OUT!*" I turned coyly to one side and bumped my hip towards the audience emphasizing the last two words making my back row timid peeps laugh and my front row hecklers cheer. In these first few moments I had told the hecklers, *yes, you exist,* and accepted where we were. I understood that the audience that was trying to be polite and made it okay for them to join in the merrymaking. I was connected to all of them and established myself as the leader. From there my set was smooth sailing.

That night when they announced the top five, I was sure I would place in at least one of those shows. I had navigated that situation expertly. I had done my absolute best. Well, I didn't. Despite how great I felt about my sets, I was still not placing in the top five on any of the shows. From what I heard the other comics muttering, the scores were all neck and neck, just tenths of a point apart from one another. I wasn't the only one doing well. After three shows and not placing, realizing I didn't actually have a chance to move forward anymore, I decided to continue my little mind trick of not looking at any of the scores. For the whole weekend, all five shows I never once saw my ranking. That piece of paper taped to the wall with all the other comics nervously hovering around it was easy to avoid. I decided those numbers were meaningless.

What good would that number do for me? It would just be an excuse to either beat myself up or feel like I was pitted against someone else. Did I need that information? Would it help me in any way? No, I decided it would not. I did not want the emotional ups and downs of looking at or considering those numbers. (Shout out to Wise Woman who gave me the strength to not look). I didn't want the opportunity to make up stories about myself or others based on those numbers. They had no bearing on my artistic output. They would tell me nothing. I decided I was not playing that game. Remember? I was playing a game with myself where all I had to do to win was feel good no matter what. And seeing the scores would not serve me in that game.

Besides, what did it matter what the judges thought of me when the audiences were having a great time? Show after show people would come up to me to congratulate me and tell me how funny I was. Flocks of women told me how emboldened they felt by my material. I had an inspiring conversation in which I got to encourage a thirteen-year-old boy who loved stand-up comedy; this was his first live show he ever attended. Fans that had come to my shows in Oakland showed up to surprise me and show support. Not only that, but one judge let me know that even though I hadn't placed that day I got the most laughs per minute of any comic on the lineup. I was clearly doing the job of making people laugh and the bonus job of inspiring them. So, really, what else was there to win?

By the end of that weekend, I may not have been moving on to the semi-finals, but I felt like I had won something more. I had won the game of feeling good no matter what. I had transcended the game and made up my own. And I had done it like a queen.

A queen doesn't waste her energy proving her power. She is power. She elicits attention and respect naturally, because she knows her real power comes from using it to get what she wants. She knows how to shine light on others, to uplift the people, to inspire entire nations to prosperity. You may laugh at the idea—*A whole nation? It'd just be great if I can get a handle on my email inbox*—but whether these nations are massive or microscopic, the point is we can run them with a magnanimous hand. If stand-up

CHAPTER XII · ATTENTION: WEARING THE CROWN

comedy has taught me anything—which I guess it has because I just wrote a whole book, *heyo!*—it's that the best service I can provide to the world is being courageous. Modeling what I want to see in the world and keeping the light coming through for myself and for everyone around me.

Wise Woman wants to let you know:

> *A queen doesn't wear a crown*
>
> *To let you know that she's a queen.*
>
> *She wears that thing*
>
> *To keep the light coming through.*

The Punchline

A Comedian, a Wise Woman, and Earthquake Woman all walk into a bar. They walk right up to you and envelop you in their essence. The comedian perches on a barstool, clutching her drink ticket. Wise Woman levitates a few inches above the sticky floor, and Earthquake Woman stands in the back as she scans the room for red flags.

Your Nice Girl is there, too, hanging out at the end of the bar, drinking a Shirley Temple so she doesn't get carried away. Her face holds a glimmer of her youth: She still rocks the round cheeks and the same hopeful eyes, but her meno-belly reveals her years as it slumps over the edge of her jeans in seeming defeat.

She's watching you and your entourage silently, clutching a glittery Valentine in her hand. It's faded and crinkled in her shaky grasp and decades old. She's confused. She thought she had it all figured out. She made a vision board. She listened to her mother. She practiced contorting so much she's got a contract with Cirque du Soleil. (She's still famous for her splits even though she's stopped wearing skirts.) She did everything she could to follow the plan and now you want her to… die? Go away?

Her hands are raw from rattling the windows. Her voice hoarse from moaning. No one hears, no one notices. And she is tired. So very tired from these attention games: the foolish romance, the war, the hiding and the seeking. And the fucked-up thing is, she's never even been to a real game, she's just sorta tailgated the whole way.

She takes in your crew of allies and silently wishes they were her fairy godmothers and could just wave a wand and give her courage, give her a heart, make her smart. Her thoughts don't go unnoticed. Empathic as hell, the Comedian, Wise Woman, and Earthquake Woman all sense her thoughts and saunter over.

Nice girl is intimidated. She should be. They're a pretty commanding presence. But she manages to stammer out a question,

"Do I really… do I really have to die?"

The Comedian laughs, "You're so dramatic! We can't kill you, even if we tried!"

"It's true," says Earthquake Woman wryly. "I've tried burning you up, but you're not flammable. Probably it's those flame-retardant jammies you're still wearing."

"Yeah, and besides, your shock at everything makes things kind of hot in the bedroom," the Comedian says salaciously. "And we know you love us, even if you don't always approve of what we do. You can't help watching, you kinky little voyeur!" The Comedian says this last part warmly as if *kinky voyeur* are the most loving words in the universe. Nice Girl blushes.

Wise Woman, who has been silently listening this whole time, reaches out and takes the crumpled Valentine from Nice Girl's hands. She unfolds it gingerly, careful not to tear it, and gazes at it thoughtfully like a mother might. Eventually she shakes her head.

"You didn't choose this," Wise Woman says. "Look, they aren't even your desires. They're your big sister's desires. Look, here's her name right here at the bottom." Nice Girl looks and her mouth falls open as she sees it right there, in the corner—a second grader's handwriting and her sister's name spelled out plain as day.

Nice Girl is dumbfounded. She has been clasping onto these desires for decades. "Well, if this isn't what I want, then what *do* I want?"

Not one of them answers. They revel in the tension of the question because they all know the fun that she's going to have figuring it out. Eventually they turn to go. As they venture towards the door, the Comedian reaches out and slips a microphone into Nice Girl's hand. Then Earthquake Woman casually walks over to her other free hand and passes her a blazing torch. And just as they're all about to disappear out the door, Wise Woman turns, smiles mischievously, and lobs a shame potato straight at Nice Girl… It plonks squarely into Nice Girl's mid-section, her muffin top softening the blow, and then falls to the floor with a dull thud. Nice Girl doesn't catch it, because her hands are full of power.

Murmuring at You from Inside My Sleeping Bag

I know, probably all you want now is for me to leave you alone so you can put on your reading glasses, look at your phone, and take a shit. I get it. The manbears and hecklers are exhausting. You deserve some alone time. But before we doze off can I just tell you a bedtime story? Or perhaps a little pep talk as you're sinking down into dreamland:

This book didn't end up in your hands for no reason. You didn't get to the last page for nothing. The world right now really is calling to you to be courageous and to become the Tempestas (and let's be honest, sexy windblown hair looks really good on you). The world needs you to storm it up and use all your skills to change the temperature right now. There are too many fools acting like kings, and whether you're a comedian or not, we all need to speak up.

We need more Empathic Queens like you who know what it means to illuminate—to share power instead of take power.

We need you to be *motherfucking weighty*.

We need you to focus.

So, when the world calls you too much, too loud, too angry, remember Earthquake Woman: You are fierce, you are powerful, you make shit happen.

When the world calls you bossy, know-it-all, or mouthy, remember you are Wise.

When the world calls you sassy, naughty, or inappropriate, remember this Comedian: You are honest, you are bold, you are loyal, persistent, and shameless.

And when things don't go the way you'd hoped, remember that it's okay because:

Your soul is secretly evolving.

Three women walk into a bar: Earthquake Woman, Wise Woman, and the Comedian.

No one sees them coming.

Acknowledgements

I would like to thank Stephanie Edd, my content editor, who challenged me to find a hundred new ways to say that "the audience laughed." Thanks for inspiring me to write better and "make it beautiful." I also want to acknowledge my developmental editor, Abigail Keyes, for wrangling the tangled web that I began with and coming up with a solid structure on which to hang this bundle of wisdom and stories. I'd also like to thank my friend and fellow writer, Jade Raybin, for pointing out my blind spots and assuming the voice of my imagined critics.

Thank you to my bestie, Joyful Raven, the "Mother of Dragons," for being interested in Earthquake Woman when she arrived during a free write in her class. Thanks for the eight-hour hangs, talking about art well into the night, being my sister in showbiz, and for midwifing the stories that were too dark for this book, but needed to be a part of the process. Most of all, thank you for believing in me.

I thank my sister, Heather Shaw, who spent hours on the phone with me when I was writing the rough draft of this book, listening to me work out my ideas, and who knows exactly how agonizingly long it took me to get my writing mojo back. And finally, I'm grateful for my mom, Linda Shaw, whom I barely mention in this book (you're welcome). You taught me how to be resilient, resourceful, speak up, and swing from vines. You are the Original Queen.

To all of the friends and fans who supported my book GoFundMe and without whom this book would not have been possible—Maxwell Houghton, Brian Dunn, Dana Olney, Rhoda Gravador, Jim Morein, Katherine Carter, Patricia Juri, Gregory Reinhardt, Hannah Romanowsky, Monique Rebelle, Sandra Lo, Jonathan Furst, Jason Toupes, Richard Jones, Yael Schy, Daniel Dechi, Libby Palomeque and Richard Ross, Alysia Schmidt, Shannon Cochran, Dan Keller, Beth Barany, Leslie Mills, Jennifer Bincarowsky, Connor Lonsdale, Melissa Eelkema, Jade Raybin, Tiffany Worthingon, Joyful Simpson, David Horwich, Sandra Williams, Josh Rigsby, Kimm Fitzgerald, Karen Buchanan, Leah Diamond, and the many supporters who wished to remain anonymous—Thank you.

The comedy business can be dark, but it just makes it that much more wonderful when you meet people who make it feel light. A final thanks goes to all of my comedy peeps. You are great people, with souls intact despite it all. Thank you for making me laugh. Thank you for believing in me. Also, please keep booking me.

Biography

photo by Nick Larson

H olly Shaw is a stand-up comedian and "hypnotherapist and performance anxiety expert" (NBC) living in Oakland, CA, and performing regularly at clubs and showcases all over the greater Bay Area. Before becoming a comedian, Shaw had spent a lifetime on stage, TV (hosted the televised *Edinburgh Revue*), and film (starring in the ABC Afterschool Special, *Love Hurts*) as an actor, professional dancer, and later as a speaker and coach. She's authored and published two prior books: *The Creative Formula* (2106) an Amazon bestseller, and *Making Art In the Middle of Madness (2020)*, a #1 New Release.

As an insatiable creative and passionate performer, Shaw embarked on an adventure from acting to dancing, to speaking, coaching, writing, and now stand-up comedy through a relentless drive to create unforgettable experiences and take audiences on a journey. Then she hit her "queen years," and her hormones started changing. Ambition turned to fatigue, and clarity to confusion as she fumbled with how to evolve and move forward. She not long discovered that stand-up comedy had changed her, made her bolder, better, and less inclined to give a fuck.

Stand-up comedy taught her to claim her space as a queen, and figured these insights should be shared with other women struggling to leap into their "queen years."

A proud single mom of a son just finishing college, Shaw tours with her stand-up show *Queen Lessons: The Comedy Special*, and hikes in the beautiful redwoods of Oakland. She has also recently entered the world of solo storytelling, performing at the Zero to Fierce Festival and the Marsh. She is working on a one-woman show. To book Holly or to learn more, please visit **www.HollyShawComedy.com** or follow her on Instagram @hollyshawcomedy.

www.ingramcontent.com/pod-product-compliance
Lightning Source LLC
Chambersburg PA
CBHW011129070526
44583CB00023B/2959